The Walk

The Walk

STEPS FOR NEW AND RENEWED
FOLLOWERS OF JESUS

STEPHEN SMALLMAN

P&R
PUBLISHING
P.O. BOX 817 • PHILLIPSBURG • NEW JERSEY 08865-0817

Italics within Scripture quotations indicate emphasis added.

Printed in the United States of America

Library of Congress Cataloging-in-Publication Data

Smallman, Stephen, 1940–
The walk : steps for new and renewed followers of Jesus / Stephen Smallman.
p. cm.
Includes bibliographical references.
ISBN 978-1-59638-093-6 (pbk.)
1. Spiritual formation. 2. Theology, Doctrinal. I. Title.
BV4511.S63 2009
248.4—dc22

2009030876

To Jack and Rose Marie Miller

Jack's vision to apply the gospel to the life of believers as well as unbelievers is the foundational principle of this book. Thank you, Lord, for the privilege of serving with Jack. I am one of a multitude of pastors whose lives and ministries were substantially impacted by the life and teaching of this unique and godly man.

Rose Marie: Your love and friendship to me, and particularly to Sandy, have given us the opportunity to see what the gospel looks like when it is lived out by a servant of Christ.

Contents

Preface

I AM PROFOUNDLY grateful to Marvin Padgett and the editors of P&R Publishing for inviting me to write a book for new believers, and supporting the approach that I have taken. My first plan was an outline of themes or doctrines that those new to the faith should understand. As you will see, however, in the writing process I found myself drawn to go in a slightly different direction and to explore the meaning of discipleship and Jesus' call to follow him. I was captivated by the simple phrase in the first verse of Mark's gospel, "the *beginning* of the gospel." This suggested to me that Mark was inviting his readers to begin the journey of discipleship through the eyes of those first disciples. I have also tried to do that, letting Scripture speak for itself as the book moves from the beginning of the gospel in Mark to the meaning of the gospel explained by Paul in Romans. I have learned, from explaining this concept to people, that there is a great need to take every believer through this kind of study. Therefore, the book keeps mentioning not only *new* disciples, but *renewed* disciples.

Writing *The Walk: Steps for New and Renewed Followers of Jesus* has given me the opportunity to pull together things I have been teaching in different settings for years. I had always sought to be a preacher of grace, but my encounter with Jack and Rose Marie Miller and my participation in the formation of World Harvest Mission served as a catalyst to show me that I should define *grace* in terms of the gospel. This book is a result of my wrestling with the implications of that idea. I appreciated the patience of participants in our Living for the King program at McLean Presbyterian Church as I kept tinkering with the program by inserting new insights I was gaining. More recently, my students in LAMPhilly, our pastoral training ministry in Philadelphia, have been my guinea pigs as I combined courses in evangelism and discipleship into one called "Making Disciples." And even more recently, a class at New Life Glenside has helped me to refine the book itself. Thank you, Dan, Lauren, Chris, Cristina, Ron, Judy, and Connie. I also appreciate Joan and Tom's assistance with the book while they were using it to help some young adults find Jesus. Will Grant gave this manuscript the most thorough "scrubbing" out of anyone who read it, and several thoughts in the book are his. As always, my wife, Sandy, has served as my first editor and most constructive critic.

The text by which I have tried to evaluate my ministry in the last several years is Acts 20:24: "However, I consider my life worth nothing to me, if only I may finish the race and complete the task the Lord Jesus has given me—the task of testifying to the gospel of God's grace." It is my prayer that this book serves that goal, and that you will come to know and love the gospel of God's grace as a result of my work.

To God be the glory!

Introduction: Meet Titus

LET YOUR IMAGINATION take you back to a few decades after the crucifixion of Christ. In the city of Rome, which was then the power center of the world, a fictional young man whom we will call Titus was searching for something more meaningful in his life. Titus had grown up accepting without question the beliefs and practices of his culture—the many gods and goddesses whose foibles were reflected in how people treated one another; the many "spiritualities" that were trying to gain followers; the growing fascination with sports and gambling as a diversion from terrible social problems such as poverty and disintegrating families. Titus had freely entered into some of the "fun" aspects of his city and had also tried out various spiritual pathways that were offered, but he was left with only a growing sense of the emptiness of his own life and the lives of those around him. He found himself growing in cynicism and indifference—attitudes that were felt throughout not only the city of Rome, but the whole Roman Empire itself.

The exception to this lack of direction and purpose was a strange group of people who were known as *followers of Jesus*. Jesus was a Jewish man who had been executed in the city of Jerusalem and according to his followers had been raised from the dead. Through an acquaintance, Titus was introduced to this group, was welcomed by them, and joined in their gatherings. The more he learned about Jesus and saw the loving character of those who were his disciples, the more Titus felt drawn in, even to the point of starting to think of himself as one of those disciples.

The primary source for the group's learning about Jesus was a short book called a *gospel* written by John Mark, a man who had grown up while Jesus lived, and whose mother was one of Jesus' earliest followers. The copy of the gospel had been given to them by one of Jesus' original disciples, Peter, who visited Rome from time to time. Titus came to love joining the group to listen to long portions of Mark being read and then hearing the elders explain the meaning. There was a power and beauty about Jesus that felt like a magnet drawing Titus to faith and a new direction for his life.

While Titus was meeting with the group, a letter arrived from another of the original leaders of the movement: the apostle Paul. Paul was known to many of the group members because they had been with him in other cities. But now Paul was planning to come to Rome, and rather than just sending a brief note to inform them of this, Paul had written a long and carefully composed letter to explain the same word used by Mark: *gospel*. Not only was there great excitement about the upcoming visit from Paul, but now the disciples in Rome had new material to study, and they eagerly read and discussed the letter now known as the epistle to the Romans.

Titus didn't understand everything he heard about Jesus, but he wanted to. He was "home," and yet not quite home. He still had not undergone baptism, a washing with water, which was the way to publicly signify that he was a disciple of Jesus. Titus came for the singing, the adoration of God through Jesus, and the teaching. But he didn't stay for the meal that the group members celebrated to remember Jesus and to receive spiritual refreshment for the challenges of their lives—lives that often included ridicule and even violence against them. Titus was at a crossroads. Was he ready to be a full member of the community that followed Jesus? Was he ready to stand up and declare himself as a disciple of this man he was only beginning to understand?

ARE YOU A TITUS?

You may be very close to the Titus I just described—new to any serious consideration of Jesus. You feel drawn to him, but you have only the vaguest idea of who he is. You are what I think of as a *new disciple*, and perhaps you are not even sure that you are a disciple. On the other hand, you may have grown up hearing about Jesus. The Bible stories about him are familiar to you—perhaps too familiar. But you have come to a place in life where you are ready for a fresh look at Jesus. Possibly some of your life experiences have shaken your faith; or perhaps, while you fully appreciate your heritage, you want to see Jesus through your own eyes, not those of your parents or church. I think of you as a *renewed disciple*. Whether you are a new or a renewed disciple, the gospel according to Mark was written to introduce you to Jesus, and that is where we will begin our study.

The scenario I have just suggested is not far from what could have been the case. The gospel according to Mark was probably the first of the accounts of the life and mission of Jesus that were called *gospels*, and strong tradition suggests that it was originally written to support the apostle Peter's early ministry in Rome. Furthermore, many in Rome were disappointed by the various spiritualities of that day and weary of the decadence and oversexualized culture of the Roman world. People were attracted to reports about this obscure man named Jesus—some considered themselves believers, and others were not ready to go that far, but they wanted to know more about this man and his teaching. The letter Paul wrote to the Romans sometime in those early years took them on additional steps into discipleship. Paul wrote assuming that they knew something about Jesus and had made some progress in following him. Those first disciples formed the church of Rome, so Paul was coming to teach the gospel *to the disciples*. As we will see, his purpose was somewhat different from Mark's, but he was still emphatic about building on the foundation of the gospel. So I will define the steps found in Paul's letter as *gospel discipleship*.

One of many terms the Bible uses to describe the life of a follower or disciple of Jesus is *walk*, which is the title I have chosen for this book. A walk can be a pleasant stroll so that we stretch our legs, or it can be a deliberate commitment to get to a destination. Obviously, the walk of following Jesus is the latter. We move toward our goal one step at a time, and that is how you should expect to walk with Jesus. Whether you are a new or a renewed disciple, your first step is to meet Jesus himself. In *The Walk* we will do that by reading the gospel written by Mark. Then we will take additional steps in discipleship through a study of Paul's letter to the church of Rome.

HOW TO USE THIS BOOK

Begin with Jesus. The only prerequisite for profiting from *The Walk* is a sincere desire to know more about Jesus. That desire includes a readiness to follow up with action steps, because it will become immediately evident in your study that Jesus is not someone to study merely as an interesting person or a key figure in history. Jesus calls us to follow him. Take your time to respond—but in the end we say either *Yes* or *No* to the call of Jesus.[1]

This is "Discipleship for Dummies." As I prepared this study, I assumed that you would be starting with no basic knowledge of Jesus and discipleship. I kept asking myself whether my words would make sense to Titus. My model was the popular For Dummies™ series of books that helped me so much in learning to use a computer. The authors of those books have never forgotten what it is like to start at the beginning. They realize that a great many of us aren't sure what button to push to turn the computer on and what to do next when strange things start happening on the computer screen. Some of us don't even know the words to use to describe what we are seeing, which means that a typical instruction manual doesn't help because even the language is new.

I began my spiritual pilgrimage over fifty years ago, just like Titus. If ever there was a "dummy" regarding things about Jesus, it was I. And I have prayed that I will never forget what it means to begin with a general belief in God and an awareness of a book that "everyone" was supposed to know about called *The Holy Bible*. Growing up in the 1950s when there was more general knowledge of religious truth, even I needed to "begin at the beginning," so I suspect that this need is even greater in

1. Appendix A contains suggestions for additional reading. This includes books and other resources for those who have basic questions of faith, such as the existence of God and the reliability of the Bible. These are very important questions for many readers, and they deserve thoughtful answers. My purpose in this book, however, is to speak to those who want to know what it means to follow Jesus.

our day. If you are a Titus, you are not alone. And don't feel intimidated by the people around you who seem to know a lot more, because if you ask them to define the "churchy" words they use, you may find out that they stumble.

This is written as a handbook, not a "complete package." If you were reading a "dummies" book about your computer, it would assume that you were looking at the computer as you read. Otherwise, what you were reading might be interesting, but it wouldn't be particularly useful until you put it into practice. In the same way, I will be calling your attention to what is written in the Bible—but this means that you need to stop and read the Bible for yourself. Ultimately I hope and pray that my book launches you on a serious study of the Bible itself, along with a growing desire to know more and more of the God who reveals himself there. And because the Bible warns about being a hearer of the Word but not a doer, you will be given assignments to help you start along the path of following Jesus. These assignments will point you in the right direction, and they are steps *you* must take. You are the one who must walk one step at a time.

Your first assignment: Buy a Bible if you don't have your own copy. I strongly recommend that you get a modern translation. I will be quoting from the New International Version (NIV), but there are many other good ones. This Bible should become a familiar companion, one that you can mark up and make notes to yourself in. If you are now part of a church, you should note the translation used in the preaching and teaching, and try to use that for your own study.

I also recommend that you start to keep a journal, at least while you study this book. You could do this in a notebook or on your computer. Try to begin a habit of writing down what you are learning and the thoughts that flow from it. Write your reactions to what you read in the Bible and to conversations with others, and even begin to write out your prayers.

Consider ways to study with others. This book is written to be used in a class, in a group, or with one or two others. Even if you don't have a leader, you should consider finding someone to do this study with you. Any learning, and particularly a study of discipleship, is far more profitable when done with others.

Take your time. To be a disciple of Jesus is a lifetime commitment. Getting started (or restarted) should be done thoughtfully. Even if you quickly read through this book, it is designed for you to go back and review and follow through on the suggested action steps. When you commit to doing the assignments at the end of each chapter, reading and studying one chapter a week may be about as fast as you will want to go. I even suggest taking a year, so that you study and discuss one chapter a month.

Summary of How to Use This Book

- Begin with a sincere desire to follow Jesus.
- Don't worry about being a "dummy."
- Get a Bible and start a journal.
- Consider ways to study with others.
- Take your time.

PART ONE

THE BASICS

The purposes for this section called "The Basics" are twofold. In the first place, I hope to give you some time to reflect on questions that lay the foundation for a study of discipleship. You can see what they are by noting the titles of the three chapters below. Being part of a church and getting started with Bible reading and prayer don't automatically make you a disciple, but these are essential tools for the life of discipleship.

But the second reason may be the more important one. While you are considering a few basic questions, you will also be introduced to Jesus by reading the gospel written by Mark. As you will see, I don't have a set reading schedule or a specific study guide. I just want to encourage you to read about and consider Jesus. If the essence of discipleship is following Jesus, then we need to know who Jesus is and what he calls us to. If we don't get that straight right from the beginning, we will quickly stray from the path. The rest is important, of course, but subsidiary to the essential truth that discipleship means following Jesus.

CHAPTER 1

What Is a Disciple?

THE UNITED STATES recently observed a grim anniversary. Forty years earlier, on April 4, 1968, Dr. Martin Luther King Jr. had been assassinated by a sniper's bullet in Memphis, Tennessee. Many newspaper and magazine articles and television specials recalled the events of that terrible day, and in almost every instance those who had been Dr. King's closest followers were interviewed about their memories. Usually they were called "disciples" of Dr. King. Most of them had gone on to further the cause of civil rights, but their accomplishments were achieved because of their relationship with and the inspiration of their leader.

Such a modern example of discipleship could be repeated over and over. I think most of us get the general idea of what it means to be a disciple. A disciple is one who is devoted to learning the ways and following the example of a teacher or master. But what about being a disciple of Jesus? That is why we are doing this study. The best place to begin our answer to that question is to read the gospel written to do just that—the gospel according to Mark.

Read Your Bible: Mark 1:1–20

(For this chapter I am including the actual text of the reading. But for the other chapters, I expect you to stop reading this book and read the suggested portion from your own Bible. If you are with others, it will be even more profitable if someone reads aloud and the rest follow along. Then talk together about what you have read. Don't get too caught up in detail—this is your introduction to Jesus, and you can come back again and again to get a fuller picture.)

The beginning of the gospel about Jesus Christ, the Son of God.

It is written in Isaiah the prophet:

> "I will send my messenger ahead of you,
> who will prepare your way"—
> "a voice of one calling in the desert,
> 'Prepare the way for the Lord,
> make straight paths for him.' "

And so John came, baptizing in the desert region and preaching a baptism of repentance for the forgiveness of sins. The whole Judean countryside and all the people of Jerusalem went out to him. Confessing their sins, they were baptized by him in the Jordan River. John wore clothing made of camel's hair, with a leather belt around his waist, and he ate locusts and wild honey. And this was his message: "After me will come one more powerful than I, the thongs of whose sandals I am not worthy to stoop down and untie. I baptize you with water, but he will baptize you with the Holy Spirit."

At that time Jesus came from Nazareth in Galilee and was baptized by John in the Jordan. As Jesus was coming up out

> of the water, he saw heaven being torn open and the Spirit descending on him like a dove. And a voice came from heaven: "You are my Son, whom I love; with you I am well pleased."
>
> At once the Spirit sent him out into the desert, and he was in the desert forty days, being tempted by Satan. He was with the wild animals, and angels attended him.
>
> After John was put in prison, Jesus went into Galilee, proclaiming the good news of God. "The time has come," he said. "The kingdom of God is near. Repent and believe the good news!"
>
> As Jesus walked beside the Sea of Galilee, he saw Simon and his brother Andrew casting a net into the lake, for they were fishermen. "Come, follow me," Jesus said, "and I will make you fishers of men." At once they left their nets and followed him.
>
> When he had gone a little farther, he saw James son of Zebedee and his brother John in a boat, preparing their nets. Without delay he called them, and they left their father Zebedee in the boat with the hired men and followed him.

Now let's think about what you just read. Even if this passage of the Bible is familiar to you, try to consider it through the eyes of our fictional friend Titus, who had no background in the teaching of the Bible. If his introduction to being a disciple was Mark, it meant that he had to jump right in and think about Jesus before anything else could be considered. The very first verse of Mark is: "The beginning of the gospel about Jesus Christ, the Son of God." The word *gospel* denotes an announcement of good news. Mark calls this the *beginning* of the gospel, so we know there will be much more to learn. But before we go any further, we need to know that the good news proclaimed in the Bible is about Jesus, who is Christ and who is the Son of God.

Time Out:

You need to know that *Christ* is not Jesus' last name. It is the Greek translation of the Hebrew word *Messiah*. *Messiah* means "an anointed one," that is, someone who had oil poured on his head making him a king. Jesus of Nazareth (his hometown) is identified as the One promised for centuries to deliver the Jewish people. So Mark identifies him as Jesus, who is *Messiah* and also the *Son of God*.

In the next few verses of Mark we are introduced to John, also called John the Baptist, who prepares the people for the coming of Messiah (another John also appears in this chapter, the fisherman who became Jesus' disciple). When John baptized Jesus, the Spirit from heaven came on him and a voice spoke from heaven, calling Jesus his beloved Son. So we are at the beginning of the gospel, and already we are learning about God the Father, God the Son, and God the Spirit—the Holy Trinity! We are also introduced to Satan, the evil one who tempts Jesus in the desert.

Obviously, we have much more to learn, but before we can think much about what has already happened, Mark immediately confronts us with the *call* of Jesus. Refer again to the portion you are reading—Jesus came into Galilee (a region in the north of Israel) "proclaiming the good news of God," which is another way of saying that he preached the gospel. Here is what he preached: "The time has come. . . . The kingdom of God is near. Repent and believe the good news!" Jesus constantly spoke and taught about the kingdom ("the kingdom of God," "the kingdom of heaven"), but notice how people were to react to this announcement of the kingdom. The word *repent* conveys the idea of turning around and is another way of speaking about converting. The turning speaks of turning to the path of following Jesus, who calls people to "believe the good news!"

The example given of converting comes in the next verses as Jesus calls four men to follow him. Simon (who also has the name *Peter*), Andrew, James, and John were all fishermen. Jesus called them to follow him, and the text says that "at once" or "without delay" they left their old life behind to follow Jesus. Is that the whole story? Probably not. Wouldn't there have been a time for these early followers to get to know Jesus? That could very well have been the case. But in terms of how Mark presents discipleship at the beginning of his gospel, a disciple is one who hears the call of Jesus and follows him. Mark gives no other details.

Consider one other example of Jesus' call to discipleship. Chapter 2 of Mark includes the account of Jesus' call to Levi, a tax collector. (Collecting taxes in the ancient world of Jesus was not a job; it was a racket in which Jews got very rich by ripping off their fellow Jews under the protection of Rome. Not surprisingly, these tax collectors were mistrusted and hated.)

Read Your Bible: Mark 2:13–17

> Once again Jesus went out beside the lake. A large crowd came to him, and he began to teach them. As he walked along, he saw Levi son of Alphaeus sitting at the tax collector's booth. "Follow me," Jesus told him, and Levi got up and followed him.
>
> While Jesus was having dinner at Levi's house, many tax collectors and "sinners" were eating with him and his disciples,

> for there were many who followed him. When the teachers of the law who were Pharisees saw him eating with the "sinners" and tax collectors, they asked his disciples: "Why does he eat with tax collectors and 'sinners'?"
>
> On hearing this, Jesus said to them, "It is not the healthy who need a doctor, but the sick. I have not come to call the righteous, but sinners."

This account is perhaps more startling than the call of the four fishermen. Jesus called out to Levi, "Follow me," and immediately Levi left his tax collector's booth to follow him. Had this man ever met Jesus? Was he already a believer? We are not told these things. All we are told is that Levi heard the call of Jesus and followed. It was a turning point in his life; Mark tells of a dinner to celebrate this new life to which all of Levi's friends were invited. (Did you notice that Jesus' companions are already called *disciples*? Check out the second paragraph of the passage.) Take another look at what Jesus had to say when people were surprised that he was associating with tax collectors and sinners: "It is not the healthy who need a doctor, but the sick. I have not come *to call* the righteous, but sinners." Here is another reference to the "call" of Jesus.

WHAT IS A DISCIPLE OF JESUS?

If we put together the lessons learned in these early chapters of Mark's telling of the gospel, I believe we can state that a disciple of Jesus is one who has *heard the call of Jesus* and has responded by *repenting*, *believing the gospel*, and *following Jesus*. Consider briefly each of those aspects of becoming a disciple of Jesus.

Hearing the Call of Jesus

As you wrestle with what it means to be a disciple of Jesus, the first thing to consider is that behind our thoughts and actions there is a mysterious working of God. It is a "God thing," as some of my friends would say. An authentic disciple is not just inspired by Jesus; he or she is *transformed* by Jesus. Those first disciples encountered the supernatural power of Jesus in their souls even as they heard the words of Jesus' call in their ears. No wonder they were compelled to leave whatever they were doing to follow! I do not think Mark would expect everyone who hears the call of Jesus to have the same experience, but I do think he is intending to teach that the end result is the same. However long it takes to get there, one who hears the call of Jesus will repent, believe the gospel, and follow Jesus because the call of Jesus includes the power to answer the call.

"Can I hear the call of Jesus today?" That is an obvious question to ask because we are no longer in a setting where Jesus is walking on the earth physically looking people in the eye and saying, "Follow me." Nevertheless, it is still the case that Jesus is calling men and women, young and old, to be his disciples—to repent, believe the gospel, and follow him. Later in our study we will see that the apostle Paul again and again refers to followers of Jesus as "the called." He was writing to people like you and me who had never personally encountered Jesus in his physical being, and yet they had experienced the call to discipleship on just as compelling a level as did those first disciples. People hear the call externally when those words of Jesus, or other portions of the Bible, are read and taught. But they also hear the call inwardly through a supernatural moving of God on their hearts and minds. We will study this idea of calling in chapter 5.

Stop and think about your experience of the call to discipleship. This may all be very new to you, as it was to Titus. On the other hand, many of you reading this have grown up with at least some knowledge of Jesus and his teaching. But along with the teaching there must be a personal and inward sense that this is for *me*. I am the one called to repent, believe, and follow. One of the most important purposes of this study is to give you the opportunity to discover whether your interest in Jesus is because of that inward and supernatural call. It is entirely possible to follow Jesus for various human-centered reasons, but such a false calling will not last, and many former "disciples" go on to try other things. But a true disciple called by Jesus will stay on that course, will "walk the walk" with all its challenges, because the call of Jesus includes the transforming power of Jesus.

Repentance

The first aspect of the call of Jesus, as recorded by Mark, is to "repent" (Mark 1:15). This aspect repeats the challenge of John the Baptist, who came "preaching a baptism of repentance for the forgiveness of sins" (1:4). To *repent* means essentially "to turn," particularly with the connotation of turning away from sin to another path. It has to do with leaving behind the old in order to follow Jesus. When I'm teaching this idea, I like to picture a room with two walls opposite each other. On one wall is the word *sin*, representing all my selfish thoughts and deeds, only a fraction of which I can really see. The opposite wall represents Jesus and the forgiveness of sin and new life found in him. I have to face one wall or the other—the life of being a disciple is never presented as *adding* Jesus to the life I am already living, but *turning* to Jesus to walk a new path.

Jesus and the other gospel preachers of the early church express the call to repentance in different ways, but they consistently challenge us to face the fact that we are sinners who need redemption—a rescue from our condition. Recall Jesus' words after the call of Levi: "I have not come to call the righteous, but sinners" (2:17). The question of sin is not a popular one to consider, but we will find ourselves returning to it again and again as the call of Jesus penetrates our souls.

Believe the Gospel

The next aspect of Jesus' call is to believe the "good news" (Mark 1:15), which is the meaning of the word *gospel.* In the setting of Mark, that gospel is the good news that God has finally come to fulfill his promise to bring salvation to the world. The term for this coming is *the kingdom of God*, which is the major theme of Jesus' teaching. Jesus announced that "the kingdom of God is *near*" (1:15), because he had come. Jesus, the Messiah, was God's coming to bring salvation to the world. Therefore, believing the gospel is another way of saying, "I believe in Jesus, who is Christ/Messiah, the Son of God."

Stop and think about how this call to believe in Jesus is the natural complement to the call to repent. The process of turning *from* our sin is at the same time the process of turning *to* Jesus. This is a true conversion—faith *and* repentance.

The call of Jesus to believe the gospel is to believe *in* him. As you read through the gospel according to Mark, you will see the new disciples grow in their faith as they learn more of Jesus. Often they will be discouraged and their faith will waver—no more so than when Jesus was crucified. But Jesus was raised from the dead, and their faith was strengthened once more.

This is a picture of the progress that you, too, will make as a disciple. The important lesson as you begin to consider the call of Jesus to believe in him is that ultimately our faith is significant because it is faith *in Jesus*, who is the Son of God, the King of the kingdom of God. We will struggle and doubt, but Jesus, the one we trust, does not.

Time Out

Don't be confused by the words *believe* and *faith.* They are the same idea: when we *believe* (a verb), we have *faith* (a noun). Both words refer to putting our trust in what we know to be true by actually taking steps to show that trust. There is an important difference between believing something to be true and believing *in* someone or something. A simple example is saying that we believe a chair will hold us up as we look at it, versus showing that we believe the chair will hold us up by sitting in it. The action of actually sitting in the chair is an expression of faith.

Come, Follow Me

The third aspect of Jesus' call to consider as you begin a study of discipleship is the call to follow him (Mark 1:17). How much of the life ahead of them did those first disciples understand? Probably very little. But when Jesus called, they followed. Mark tells the gospel story in a way that makes it quite clear that believing in Jesus means following Jesus as his disciple.

Consider one other portion of Jesus' teaching in Mark as you think about the call to follow. About halfway through Mark's gospel, the focus changes, and Jesus begins to move toward the time of his crucifixion.

Read Your Bible: Mark 8:27–34

> Jesus and his disciples went on to the villages around Caesarea Philippi. On the way he asked them, "Who do people say I am?"
>
> They replied, "Some say John the Baptist; others say Elijah; and still others, one of the prophets."
>
> "But what about you?" he asked. "Who do you say I am?"
>
> Peter answered, "You are the Christ."
>
> Jesus warned them not to tell anyone about him.
>
> He then began to teach them that the Son of Man must suffer many things and be rejected by the elders, chief priests and teachers of the law, and that he must be killed and after three days rise again. He spoke plainly about this, and Peter took him aside and began to rebuke him.
>
> But when Jesus turned and looked at his disciples, he rebuked Peter. "Get behind me, Satan!" he said. "You do not have in mind the things of God, but the things of men."
>
> Then he called the crowd to him along with his disciples and said: "If anyone would come after me, he must deny himself and take up his cross and follow me."

"Take up [your] cross and follow me." The passage begins with an affirmation that Jesus is the Christ, the Messiah. That was a remarkable confession for a Jewish person to make, but Peter (remember, *Peter* is another name for *Simon*) was very clear in what he said. This is where Mark began his gospel, as we have seen, and Peter as well as the other disciples have now embraced this affirmation personally. Notice that after Peter's confession Jesus "*began* to teach" something new. He called himself the "Son of Man," a title for Messiah, and explained that he must suffer many things, culminating in his death. Then he added something that was totally confusing to the disciples until after it happened—he said that three days after his death, he would rise again.

Clearly, the idea of Jesus' dying was not to Peter's liking, and he argued with Jesus and even rebuked him. But then Jesus spoke of what that meant for his disciples: "If anyone would come after me, he must deny himself and take up his cross and *follow me*" (Mark 8:34). The call that we saw in chapter 1, to follow him, is repeated, but Jesus has now added that a disciple must be prepared to follow him even in his death (which is the meaning of the cross). This is not something that any of us want to hear, but the gospel message is very clear: following Jesus will not be easy; there will be sacrifices to be made, possibly even loss of our lives for him. Jesus explains this idea further in the next portion of the teaching (8:35–38), which you will read later. There are many more lessons about what it means to follow Jesus, but the reality of his cross and our death with him dominates the challenge of being a disciple.

I Will Make You Fishers of Men

This has been a long answer to a basic question: "What is a disciple of Jesus?" But one other truth must be considered from those first verses in Mark. Jesus came to this earth with a mission. He was sent to fulfill the mission given to him by his Father in heaven: to bring the kingdom of God. Therefore, an important part of the call to discipleship is a call to join him on that mission. He said to those first disciples, "Follow me, . . . and I will make you fishers of men" (Mark 1:17). When we remember that he was speaking to fishermen, we can appreciate that he was calling them to be devoted to working with people instead of fish. We are called to follow Jesus—to repent and believe in him—but in following Jesus, we now join him in the great work he came to do. We will return to discuss this mission more fully in the last chapter of this study, but it is important to see that Mark includes this idea at the very beginning of his gospel.

Summary of Chapter 1

The purpose of this chapter was to introduce you to Jesus and his call to discipleship—to follow him. We did this by thinking about how Mark begins the gospel.

Who is Jesus?

- He is Christ, the Messiah, also called Son of Man.
- He is the Son of God.
- He was baptized with water and then with the Spirit from heaven.
- He came to do battle with Satan and his demons.
- He preached the gospel—the good news that the kingdom of God was near.

What is a disciple of Jesus?

- One who has heard the call of Jesus and has responded by:
    - Repenting.
    - Believing the gospel.
    - Following Jesus.

Assignments

1. **Read Mark.** The first assignment for this study of discipleship is to begin your reading of the Bible. If possible, set aside time to read the entire gospel of Mark in one sitting or in just a few days. Try to read it through quickly to take in the whole story.

2. **Read Mark 1–3.** Then start again and focus on chapters 1–3 and Jesus' first weeks with the disciples. Plan to have read the entire gospel a second time by the time you complete chapter 3 of *The Walk*. As you read, remind yourself: *That's me. I'm the one watching him heal a leper or cast out demons. I see him praying and teaching and proclaiming the forgiveness of sin.* And ask yourself: *What am I to make of all this? And what does it mean to follow such a Master?*

3. **Begin your journal.** Get a simple notebook or use your computer, and start to write your thoughts and questions that come to you as you read. These can be private thoughts or good things to talk about when you meet with your mentor or group.

CHAPTER 2

Do I Have to Go to Church?

THEY LIKE JESUS *but Not the Church*[1] is the title of a recent book describing the fact that people all over the world continue to find an attraction to Jesus but are turned off by various expressions of Jesus' church. So a natural question comes up: "If I become a disciple of Jesus, do I have to go to church?" The short answer to that question is *YES!*

Obviously, that answer will require more explanation. When I said "go to church," that was to get your attention—there is much more to church than simply attending a church service somewhere. I'm sure that many of you reading this have not had very good experiences with the church. The title of that book says it very well. Perhaps you thought you could consider being a disciple of Jesus apart from the church. But you can't, and this is such an important matter that I am

1. Dan Kimball, *They Like Jesus but Not the Church* (Grand Rapids: Zondervan, 2007).

making it the first thing I talk about after introducing you to the basic idea of discipleship.

WHAT IS THE CHURCH?

Think about this: most of you reading this book have come to this study as a result of some encounter with Jesus' church. Like the imaginary situation of Titus, you have probably met some believers in your quest for faith. You may be doing this study as part of a class or small group. I have interviewed many people about how they became disciples of Jesus, and the great majority have come to that place in their lives as a result of contact and communication with others who follow Christ. Being a disciple of Jesus is a *personal* response to the call of Jesus, but we are also called to become part of a *community*, a *fellowship*, of disciples. This is the essence of the church that Jesus came to build.

In the first lesson on discipleship, you read from Mark that Peter confessed, "You are the Christ" (Mark 8:29). When Matthew tells about that same incident, he adds more of what Jesus said at that time. (*Matthew* is another name for *Levi*, the tax collector whom Jesus called to follow him.)

Read Your Bible: Matthew 16:13–28

(Remember, by now I'm assuming that you have your own copy of the Bible to read. So stop here and open your Bible to Matthew, which is the book that comes before Mark, and read the passage. You have probably figured it out by now, but the first number refers to the chapter and the second number to the verse within the chapter. The whole Bible is divided into chapters and verses to make it easier to find a particular text, but those breaks are not in the original, so don't be surprised when a thought takes you into the next verse or even the next chapter.)

Notice that after Peter made his confession, Jesus said, "I tell you that you are Peter, and on this rock I will build my church, and the gates of Hades will not overcome it" (Matt. 16:18). The word *church* means "a congregation or assembly." The Hebrew people had been God's church, so the word was not new. But now Jesus declares his intention to build "*my* church." This was new. He would build it on Peter the rock (usually understood to mean Peter and the other apostles as they confess Jesus as Messiah and Son of God). Later you will read of the church's being built on the foundation of the apostles and prophets, but the builder is Jesus, and even the "gates of Hades" (another word for *hell*) will not stop the advance of Jesus' church.

Time Out

Apostles or Disciples?

By now in your reading of Mark, you should have come to chapter 3 and the appointment of the twelve apostles (3:13–19). These apostles would become the leaders of the church after Jesus' time on earth. The word *apostle* means "sent one," or "sent on a mission." But Jesus chose the apostles from among his *disciples*. The unique calling of apostle was fulfilled in the founding of the church and the writing of the New Testament portion of the Bible, but *disciple* continues to be the term that identifies followers of Jesus to this day.

ARE CHRISTIANS ALWAYS DISCIPLES?

You may have noticed that I have not yet used the word *Christian* to talk about disciples. Unfortunately, *Christian* has lost its original meaning and can mean almost anything people want. In the perspective of many, even those already in the church, there is actually a difference between a Christian and a disciple. You may have this idea yourself. Can you be a Christian without being a disciple of Jesus? Do you think of discipleship as some kind of advanced Christian commitment?

Jesus and the writers of the New Testament make no distinction between a disciple and a Christian. The word *disciple* is used over 200 times in the four gospel accounts. The word *Christian* means "belonging to Christ" and was first used to describe the members of the church of Antioch (in what is modern-day Syria). The New Testament book of Acts, which tells the history of the early years of Jesus' church, makes this comment: "The disciples were called Christians first at Antioch" (Acts 11:26).

Therefore, I will continue to use the term *disciple* or *follower of Jesus*, but this is not any different from *Christian*, when that word is properly understood. A Christian church must be understood as a community of disciples of Jesus. That community takes many forms; churches come in all sizes and "brands," but at the core there must be the commitment to follow Jesus. That is one important clue to what can go wrong with a church—when it loses its fundamental calling to be a community of Jesus' disciples. Churches become institutions, existing to preserve their own organizations and traditions, when the focus is on the church itself instead of Jesus.

When I started the chapter by saying, "Yes, a disciple must go to church," this is what I was talking about. You need to be part of a community of disciples where you learn to follow Jesus together with others. It won't be a perfect church, because it will be made up of disciples who are struggling—just like you.

HOW DOES THE CHURCH HELP YOU GROW AS A DISCIPLE?

Now you may ask, "How do I know *which* church?" From the handful of early disciples, Jesus' church has grown to become the largest single religious group in the world. Most places in the world these days have many choices of churches, and perhaps in your search for the right one you have been disappointed again and again. Here is a list of four things a healthy church does to help you grow as a disciple. Ask God to send you to a community of disciples where you find these things taking place.

The Church Is Where You Publicly Confess Faith in Jesus

Think about our friend Titus. He felt very welcome to sit in with the church as the disciples studied Mark and as they sang and prayed. But he also realized that there needed to come a time when he would publicly declare himself to be a follower of Jesus. When he was ready to do this, it would come by way of a washing ceremony called *baptism*. As we saw from Mark, baptism came from John the Baptist (and the ritual probably appeared even earlier than John). But Jesus gave baptism a distinctive role as the way in which people were to declare themselves to be his disciples and become part of the community of his disciples. After he was raised from the dead, Jesus sent his disciples out to "make disciples of all nations," and the first step in fulfilling that commission was "baptizing them in the name of the Father and of the Son and of the Holy Spirit" (Matt. 28:16–20).

In the history of Jesus' church, one of the most important ministries to new disciples has been their preparation for baptism. This has been done in many different ways, but it has usually included instruction in the basics of faith and the opportunity to make an oral confession along with the ceremony of baptism. The ceremony itself has been done in many ways (pouring or sprinkling water on the person, immersing a person in the water, and so on), and unfortunately this has been one source of division within the church. Yet baptism allows the church to celebrate with a new disciple and to pledge to help that person stay on the path of following Jesus.

Time Out

The Apostles' Creed

In the early church a form of confession gradually became standardized into what is known as the Apostles' Creed. In a day when most people couldn't read, and books such as the Bible were very expensive and hard to find, this creed helped early Christians remember and defend the basics of their new faith in Jesus. This creed is now confessed by all branches of the Christian church (this is the meaning of *catholic* in the creed), but originally it was a personal confession before a person was baptized. On the next page is a widely used version of the creed for you to study and memorize.

I believe in God the Father Almighty,
Maker of heaven and earth.

I believe in Jesus Christ, his only Son, our Lord,
who was conceived by the Holy Spirit,
and born of the virgin Mary.
He suffered under Pontius Pilate,
was crucified, died, and was buried;
he descended into hell.[2]
The third day he rose again from the dead.
He ascended into heaven
and is seated on the right hand of God the Father Almighty.
From there he will come to judge the living and the dead.

I believe in the Holy Spirit,
the holy catholic church,
the communion of saints,
the forgiveness of sins,
the resurrection of the body,
and the life everlasting. Amen.

The Church Is Where You Will Find Spiritual Support and Nourishment

Once people made a public confession of being a follower of Jesus, as represented by baptism, they would be welcome to join the rest of the church in taking part in a special meal that Jesus gave his church. It is often called the *Lord's Supper* or *communion.*

2. "Hell" in the creed is usually understood to mean the place where all dead people go and is repeated "to make the point that life left his body and he died as really, truly, and completely as you and I must expect in due course to do." J. I. Packer, *Affirming the Apostles' Creed* (Wheaton, IL: Crossway Books, 2008), 20.

Just before his crucifixion, Jesus established this ceremonial meal to represent the ongoing spiritual life of his church.

Read Your Bible: Mark 14:22–26

Notice how each aspect of communion could be expanded to discuss the life of the church in its ministries of worship and teaching and service. We are sustained by fellowship with Jesus (pictured by actually eating and drinking the bread and wine); we do this with one another (*communion* has the same root idea as *community*); and we repeat this meal over and over as long as we are on this earth, because our need to be in fellowship with Jesus and one another will only grow as we grow as disciples.

There is certainly a great deal more to be said about the church as the place to grow spiritually. This is often described as "spiritual formation," when we grow closer to Christ personally and as a community.[3] But it is enough for a new or renewed disciple at this point in our study to know that without a church you will struggle in your desire to follow Jesus. In settings such as the one represented by Titus, baptism marked the point at which a disciple "joined the church"—which means submitting to the community's direction and discipline as the way to move forward as a disciple of Jesus.

For Reflection

What does this submission look like in your situation? Have you joined a church—not just the formality of membership, but serious commitment to follow Jesus with the community?

3. Appendix A, "Further Reading," contains several suggestions for basic books and other resources to help in your spiritual formation.

The Church Is Home Base for Serving Jesus by Loving Our Neighbors

Keep in mind that fundamental to discipleship is serving others and reflecting the compassion of Jesus to those in need. We are to pass along the good news that he proclaimed, and we also pass along the light that has come into our lives because of Jesus. This goes back to Jesus' original challenge: "Come, follow me, . . . and I will make you fishers of men" (Mark 1:17). Don't miss the fact that Jesus said he would *make us* fishers of men. This will take some work on Jesus' part. We are selfish, self-centered people. Where do we find help in serving others? It is in the church, the community of disciples. This is where we will find opportunities to serve one another, and it is also where we join with others in reaching out. None of us feels adequate to be "fishers of men" in ourselves. When we reach out as a community, however, we can make a real difference. That is why I speak of the church as "home base" for loving our neighbors.

Don't wait until you make a confession of faith to love your neighbors. I can think of several examples of people being drawn to Jesus by first participating in projects of love and care sponsored by churches. One friend went with a church group to fix up a day-care center in a poor neighborhood. He was moved by the fact that the members of the group were giving up a Saturday to help others, contrary to his own pattern of selfishness. But more than that, he discovered a depth of love and commitment that he knew he didn't have. It was several years before he actually gave his life to Jesus, but his journey toward becoming a disciple of Jesus started with spending a Saturday at the day-care center.[4]

4. This is the story of Bill that I tell in chapter 5 of my book *Spiritual Birthline: Understanding How We Experience the New Birth* (Wheaton, IL: Crossway Books, 2006).

The Church Is the Place to Raise a Family in Christ

When we repent, believe the gospel, and follow Jesus, it impacts every aspect of our lives. We follow Jesus in the way we treat others, in the way we do business, and in the way we live ordinary daily lives.[5] One of the most important areas in which this truth expresses itself is the matter of our families. If you are a disciple of Jesus, you will want a husband or wife who is following Jesus with you. If God gives you children, you will want to have those children join you so that you are following Jesus as a family. Take a moment and read about how important marriage and children were to Jesus.

Read Your Bible: Mark 10:1–16

Other biblical passages teach that divorce may happen in extreme situations. Jesus understands how hard our hearts can become, and he has come to bring new life to the messes we make of our lives. But in these verses it is very clear that he supports the original design of marriage ("what God has joined together, let man not separate," v. 9). It is also clear that he has a special love for children who are brought to him for blessing ("for the kingdom of God belongs to such as these," v. 14). If you are a disciple who is married or wants to marry, Jesus says to you *and your family* (the Bible often refers to the family as "household"[6]), "Follow me."

It is Jesus' church that will offer the support and encouragement to raise up families that are centered in Christ. From

5. This is explained more fully in chapter 11, "The Gospel Changes Everything."

6. One of the greatest affirmations about families came from Joshua, who was Moses' successor: "As for me and my household, we will serve the LORD" (Josh. 24:15).

the first day of its existence, the church has welcomed people to bring their children along (Acts 2:38–41). In fact, for most of its history the church has baptized the children of believers to symbolize that truth (although not all churches agree with the practice). It is also in the church that those who are single will have the opportunity to love and be part of the discipleship of children, and single parents will be supported in their struggle.

IT ALL SOUNDS GOOD—BUT GET REAL!

I have deliberately given a profile of what Jesus' church *should be*. Most of us know that none of our churches totally live up to that profile. But before you dismiss this chapter and look for alternatives to the church, you need to know that there are many, many examples of wonderful churches that are passionate about honoring and representing Christ, where you will learn to follow Jesus and grow in understanding and service. Again, of course, you will never find the perfect church. The joke often told is that if you did find the perfect church, it wouldn't want you—because then it would no longer be perfect!

It is my assumption that most of you are reading this book on discipleship because someone gave you the book or invited you to join a group to study together. That means you are already encountering a community of disciples, which is the essence of Jesus' church. Look around the group and get to know the people. The goal is to grow *together* as disciples of Jesus. You need them, but they need you, too, even if you are still wondering whether you should call yourself a disciple. Share your struggles. Ask your questions. See if you don't meet Jesus in the lives of others.

Summary of Chapter 2

I asked whether you had to "go to church" to be a disciple. And the answer was *YES!*

But then I asked, "What is the church?"

- It is the community of disciples that Jesus promised he would build.
- It is built on the foundation of the apostles.
- It was seeing how disciples lived together in a church that first gave them the label *Christian*.

How does the church help you grow as a disciple?

- It is where you will publicly confess Jesus (baptism).
- It is where you will find spiritual support and nourishment (communion).
- It is your home base for serving others in the name of Jesus.
- It is where you will raise a Christian family.

Assignments

1. **Continue reading Mark.** Before you complete this first part of the study ("The Basics"), you should try to read Mark at least twice. You are being introduced to Jesus and his work. As Mark says, this is the gospel, so try to grow in familiarity with his presentation of the gospel even as you begin to read in other places in the Bible.

2. **Continue to write in your journal.** Are you starting a habit of writing down your thoughts as you read and reflect? This may be where you keep notes from class sessions if you are

studying with others. Soon it will be interesting to go back and see how you are growing in understanding.

3. **Write about the church.** Use your journal to put down your own thoughts about what the church should be, and your own experiences with the church. If you are not in a church or in one that points you to Jesus, begin to pray that you will find a church home.

CHAPTER 3

Learning to Read the Bible and Pray

WOULDN'T IT BE AMAZING to learn to be a disciple by actually walking along with Jesus, as those first disciples did? We could hear him speak, watch him in action, and speak to him whenever we wanted. On the one hand, it is true that we don't have that exact experience, but on the other hand, we can hear the words of Jesus and see him in action and speak to him whenever we want to—this is because we have the Bible and prayer.

For the third lesson on the basics of discipleship, I want you to think about these two "tools." I believe that the church, the community of disciples that we talked about in chapter 2, is the most important single aid to being Jesus' disciple. But learning to read the Bible and learning to pray are almost as important. In fact, if the church fulfills its calling, that will include teaching people to read the Bible and to pray.

THE BIBLE

I don't like to read. I haven't read a book in years. In this age of computers and computer games, people are losing the habit of reading and thinking about what they read. These are the kinds of things we hear very commonly, and perhaps you are saying the same thing. Yet if you are becoming serious about being a disciple of Jesus, you need to get back to the books, and particularly the Book. If you are reading this, it means you *can* read. The next step is to *want* to read. If this needs to change for you, pray and ask God to give you a new desire and a new *discipline* (doesn't that word sound close to *disciple*? It is the same root) to read.

Don't forget that many people in the world can't read. "Reading the Bible" may mean listening carefully as someone else reads aloud. For example, one of the most effective means of telling the world about Jesus has been the *Jesus* film, which is the gospel according to Luke, read and dramatized.[1] People can certainly become disciples of Jesus without knowing how to read, but one way or another they must hear the gospel. If you can read, don't take for granted what a gift you have been given.

Explore the Book

The Bible is often thought of as a book, but it is better to consider it as a library or a collection of books. The Bible contains sixty-six books, divided into the Old Testament, with thirty-nine books, and the New Testament, with twenty-seven books. The division between the testaments is simply those books written *before* the coming of Jesus and those written *after*. The Old Testament tells the story of God's dealing with the Hebrew people

1. Learn more about the *Jesus* film at www.jesusfilm.org.

(Jews), and the New Testament presents Jesus and the early years of Jesus' disciples' going to the world with the gospel.

Take some time and explore this remarkable Book. Check the table of contents and notice that the thirty-nine books of the Old Testament actually form most of the Bible. Locate the point in your Bible between Malachi (the last book of the Old Testament) and Matthew (the first book of the New Testament). You can see for yourself that about four-fifths of the Bible is Old Testament. The longest book of the Bible is Psalms, which you will find in the center part of the Bible. It is the only book originally written in separate chapters.

Time Out

Doesn't everyone already know all this?

If you grew up in a church, you may be getting impatient with me, thinking that I'm taking the "dummies" theme too far. Trust me—many other readers (even some who grew up in a church) are saying, "Thank you; I needed someone to help me start from the very beginning." I speak from my own experience. I grew up in an educated American family, but even this elementary introduction to the Bible was completely new to me. Don't be ashamed to call yourself a beginner—just don't let that hold you back from becoming a *learner*. That is a key ingredient of being a disciple, and we all have to start somewhere.

You could spend a lifetime studying the Bible and never take it all in. But you can start, which is why we picked one book,

Mark, and just jumped in. You will find that little by little you will gain a better grasp of the Bible as a whole, but the best way to do that is to focus serious attention on one portion of the Bible and then another. This is another reason why you need to be in a church that centers on Jesus and will teach you the Bible.

The Big Story

While the Bible is a collection of sixty-six books, it is at the same time one Book, telling one story, threaded through many smaller stories. The big story tells about God's relationship to man and unfolds in four parts:

- *Creation*, which was God's making all things, including the man and woman, and calling it all "very good" (Gen. 1:31). The Bible starts out: "In the beginning, God created . . ." (1:1). God was already present, but everything else had a beginning.
- *Fall*, when mankind sinned and brought a curse on the earth. The man and woman were alienated from God, but also from each other. The story of Adam and Eve's eating the fruit is not trivial—it was the choice to defy God's clear command to follow their own desires (Gen. 3). This is still the essence of sin.
- *Redemption*, which teaches that God removes the curse to restore *shalom* (peace) to his creation. His promise of redemption began in Genesis 3 with the shedding of animals' blood to cover Adam and Eve with their skins and the promise to crush the head of the serpent (Gen. 3:15). He promised through the prophets to send a King to rule with justice and righteousness. In time he sent his own Son

to earth as our Redeemer to fulfill that promise through his death and resurrection.

- *Consummation*, when God will bring his creation, including mankind, to the glory that he originally intended for it. That glory is found in Christ, but the fullness of that glory will come in the future, at the return of Christ to the earth.

When I explain the big story of the Bible, I draw out a series of lines all gradually coming together at a single point. The first segment looks like a pyramid without a top. That is the Old Testament. There are accounts of fascinating individuals, priests and sacrifices, covenants, journeys through the wilderness, and the like, but the story is never complete. The Old Testament ends with the prophet Malachi's telling people to wait until "the sun of righteousness will rise with healing in its wings," and to listen for the voice of "the prophet Elijah" calling them to turn around (repent) before the day of judgment (Malachi 4—the last chapter of the Old Testament).

Fig. 1. The biblical pyramid

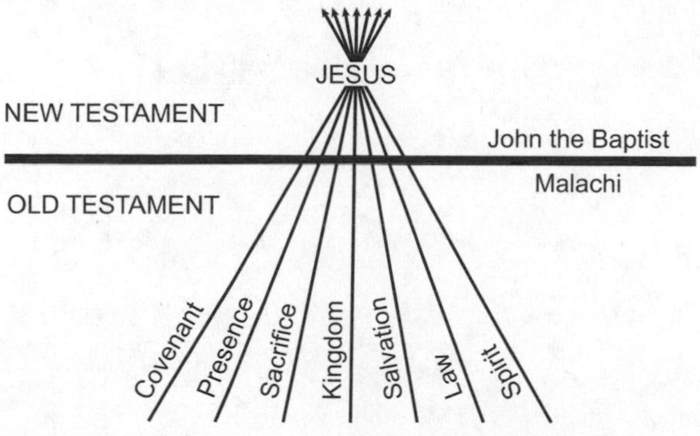

The New Testament is the top of the pyramid. It simply pulls together all the strands of the Old Testament and shows how they are fulfilled in the coming and ministry of Jesus. You have already begun to see this cohesion in your reading of Mark. Mark begins where Malachi ended with that "voice" calling out, "Prepare the way for the Lord" (Mark 1:1–8). Jesus later explained that John the Baptist was the Elijah prophesied in Malachi (Matt. 11:11–15). When Jesus began his public ministry, after his baptism, he announced, "The time has come . . ." (Mark 1:15)—in other words, the coming of the kingdom of God is the fulfillment of all the promises of the Old Testament. The long wait is over. This is *good news* indeed![2]

Of course, it gets much more involved than what I have described. But if you keep in mind this big story as you begin to expand your reading in the Bible, the smaller stories will make more and more sense. For one of your assignments I will ask you to sample this big story by reading the first chapters of the Bible and the last chapters. You can see the four themes of the big story—*creation*, *fall*, *redemption*, and *consummation*—begun and then fulfilled. In that reading, the first creation makes way for the new creation, the curse from the first creation is taken away, and once more mankind is eating from the tree of life.

The Authority of the Bible—God's Word

Disciples of Jesus have always given special respect to the authority of the Scriptures (another term for the Bible). Followers of Jesus call the Holy Bible "God's Word" because they

2. A recent book giving an overview of the whole Bible begins with a chapter on the resurrection of Jesus. That is right—the "big story" makes sense in the light of the triumph of Jesus over sin and death. Michael D. Williams, *Far as the Curse Is Found* (Phillipsburg, NJ: P&R Publishing, 2005).

believe that God has spoken in a unique way through the various authors inspired to write the Bible.

Of course, skeptics will question viewing the Bible this way. This skepticism has recently become visible through a popular novel and movie, *The Da Vinci Code*, and publicity surrounding the release of an ancient book called *The Gospel of Judas*. This kind of challenge is nothing new. In a short time people will forget these challenges when the next attempt to debunk the Bible comes along, but in the end the Bible will still stand.

You, too, may have questions about the uniqueness and divine inspiration of the Bible. You should feel free to explore these questions, but the most constructive approach will be to start with help from people who also respect the Bible (another reason why you need a good church). I will suggest some sources in the "Further Reading" section (Appendix A) at the back of the book. But the best way to resolve questions about the Bible is just to read it. This is a Book like no other, and you need to discover that truth for yourself.

Disciples of Jesus receive the Bible as God's Word for one primary reason: because Jesus did. We need to have Jesus' view of the Bible. Let me point you to just two examples of that view.

Read Your Bible: Mark 12:35–37

These verses describe the debate between Jesus and religious leaders in the days just before the crucifixion. In this example Jesus is asking them how the Messiah could be a son of David when David calls him "Lord" in Psalm 110. Notice particularly how Jesus introduces that quotation of the Bible in verse 36: "David himself, *speaking by the Holy Spirit*, declared . . ." Jesus assumed that when he was quoting the Bible, even though written by a human author such as David, it was the Holy Spirit speaking—it was, literally, the word of God.

For the second example, read about the temptation of Jesus just after his baptism. Mark just mentions it (1:12–13), but in their gospels, both Matthew (Matt. 4:1–11) and Luke (see below) give an expanded description.

Read Your Bible: Luke 4:1–13

Notice in the reading that three times Satan tempts Jesus, and all three times Jesus answers by quoting from the Bible ("it is written"; "it says"). Keep in mind the big story. Jesus finds himself in the same position as Adam and Eve when they faced Satan in the garden of Eden—being tempted to fulfill hunger by denying what God had said (Gen. 3:1–5). Whereas the first Adam (and Eve) chose the promise of Satan over the word of God, Jesus, the second Adam (as he is called later in the New Testament), obeyed the word of God and defeated Satan. This is the gospel—Jesus' doing for us what we have failed to do for ourselves. It is also worth noting that by the end of the temptations, Satan himself is quoting the Bible (Luke 4:10–11). Here is a powerful reminder that biblical quotations can be used to prove almost anything we want. This is a further reminder that an important part of growing as a disciple is learning to become a wise interpreter of the Bible.

Practical Questions

The Bible is an ancient document. Moses was the first author, possibly as early as 1400 BC, and the Bible was finished before the end of the first century AD. Most of the Old Testament was written in Hebrew and the New Testament in Greek. That means that what you and I read are copies and translations of the original writings. The story of how the Bible was preserved and meticulously copied and translated is remarkable. Don't be surprised, however, that occasionally you learn that scholars have some question about which copy or manuscript is most accurate.[3] These quibbles are reminders that whereas the Bible as originally given was divinely inspired, the translations we read are trustworthy but not perfect.

I repeat my advice: the best way to deal with questions about the Bible is just to read it. Develop a habit of regularly reading the Bible for yourself, and participate in groups where you study the Bible.

PRAYER

Do you pray? Everyone prays in one way or another. If you ever call out, "O God!" even in anger, you are praying. A curse is a perverse form of prayer. Think about all the ways in which prayer comes up in ordinary conversation (such as "our thoughts and prayers are with you"). In one sense, prayer is natural to every human being. Prayer is universal in the human race. Because we are made in God's image, even though sin is very present in all our lives, an inner witness still calls us to speak to the God who made us. "Being spiritual" is part of who we are.

The challenge for those who become disciples of Jesus is not the idea of prayer, but how to learn to pray in a way that

3. You have already encountered this kind of question in your reading of Mark. Mark probably ends with 16:8, but later copies added endings that seemed to make the gospel more complete. Most modern translations include one of those endings but explain that the ending of Mark is a problem.

honors God—prayer that Jesus would support and encourage. How do we learn to repent of bad praying when it is only for selfish purposes, and turn to godly praying?

Like the Bible, prayer is a vast topic, and one that Jesus had a great deal to say about. Learn to use the Bible as your primary prayer book (for example, most of the psalms are prayers). The best place to learn how to pray is at gatherings with other believers. Listen to the public prayers during worship services and the prayer time in smaller groups. Pray along in your heart. When you say "Amen" at the end of others' prayers, you are saying to the Lord, "I agree—that is my prayer, too." There will come a time when you feel ready to orally add your prayers to those of the other group members. Just a sentence or two can be a meaningful addition to the shared time of prayer.

You must also learn to pray privately. Jesus has given us a "beginners' prayer," and for this introduction to the basics of discipleship, it is the best place to start. In a famous passage in the gospel written by Matthew, called the "Sermon on the Mount" (Matt. 5–7), Jesus presents what it means to live in his kingdom, and one important part of kingdom living is prayer. The actual prayer Jesus taught, in Matthew 6:9–13, is popularly known as the *Lord's Prayer* (also known as the *Our Father*) and is perhaps the most famous prayer in the world.

I called the Lord's Prayer a "beginners' prayer" because it is a wonderful place to start. But it is much more than that. No matter how much you advance in a life of prayer, you will never outgrow this basic prayer. What I will explain to you about using the Lord's Prayer is a practice I started many years ago to help me stop struggling with my praying—and I have never found a better guide to prayer and still follow it to this day. This is one gift that keeps on giving.

Read Your Bible: Matthew 6:5–15

If you have had any exposure to Christian teaching, you have heard of this prayer and have probably repeated it yourself in church services or other settings. In fact, it often happens that when a person becomes serious about being a disciple of Jesus, one of the things that he or she does is to reject the Lord's Prayer because it is too familiar and has been repeated over and over, almost as magic (the very "babbling" that Jesus warned against in verse 7). Don't do that! This teaching of Jesus is a remarkable gift and will give you a good foundation in learning to pray. Here are several steps that will form that foundation:

Memorize the Lord's Prayer

I recommend that you learn a traditional form of the Lord's Prayer, since it is the one you will recite together with other disciples when you are together in worship.[4] Here is one traditional version; note that I divide it up in a way that will help you use it to guide your praying:

> Our Father, who art in heaven,
> Hallowed be thy Name.
> Thy kingdom come; thy will be done on earth as it is in
> heaven.
> Give us this day our daily bread.
> And forgive us our debts, as we forgive our debtors.[5]
> And lead us not into temptation, but deliver us from evil.

4. You can read a shorter version of the Lord's Prayer in Luke 11:2–4. This was taught in a different setting from Matthew 6, which suggests that Jesus taught this prayer many times during his ministry.

5. Another traditional version of the prayer says here: "And forgive us our trespasses, as we forgive those who trespass against us." It is the same idea.

(For thine is the kingdom, and the power, and the glory,
forever.[6] Amen.)

Use the Lord's Prayer

Look again at the prayer and notice that it teaches us how we can speak to God ("*Our Father*, who art in heaven") and then lists five different things we ask. The traditional ending, "For thine is the kingdom, and the power, and the glory, forever," is appropriate to include at the end of your prayer, but it was not part of the original prayer that Jesus taught.

Picture the prayer as a hand—"Our Father" is the palm and the requests are the five fingers. As you are learning to use the Lord's Prayer to guide you, you can touch each part of the hand as you pray. I have found it very helpful to repeat the traditional words of the prayer and then add in my own prayer. This means that I pray, "Our Father, who art in heaven," and I stop to express what it means to be so intimate with Almighty God. I am speaking to him as Jesus did—as *Father*. When I touch the palm of my hand, it reminds me that just as my fingers are connected through my palm, everything else I have to say to God grows out of this privilege given to me by Jesus. Then I touch the first finger and pray the first request, "Hallowed be thy Name," and I use my own words to express my adoration and honor of God.

This is how I work through each part of the prayer. Do you see how each of the five requests opens the way to speak to God personally? They also provide an order given to us by Jesus. For example, we pray for God's honor and kingdom *before* we pray for our own needs. You will learn that once you have stepped

6. Or "for ever and ever."

Fig. 2. The hand reaching to heaven

through the prayer, you will have covered almost everything that you wanted to pray about—and probably some things you wouldn't have even thought of.

- *Hallowed be thy Name*—a time to worship and pray for the honor of God.
- *Thy kingdom come; thy will be done on earth as it is in heaven*—a time to pray for the expansion of Jesus' rule in our hearts and in the world, and for that day when he will come to finish the work of the kingdom.[7]
- *Give us this day our daily bread*—a time to pray for personal concerns such as food, health, and work for ourselves and others.

7. Some teaching of the Lord's Prayer makes "thy will be done on earth as it is in heaven" a separate request. I use it as a definition of "thy kingdom come."

- *And forgive us our debts, as we forgive our debtors*—a time to confess our sin but also to look at broken relationships and pray for restoration and forgiveness.

- *And lead us not into temptation, but deliver us from evil*—a time to pray for guidance and protection as we take on the challenges of a new day.

Summary of Chapter 3

Two basic tools will enable us to follow Jesus as new or renewed disciples: learning how to read the Bible and learning how to pray.

The Bible:

- Explore the Book—it is more of a library than a single book.
- The big story—all those books tell a single story:
    - Creation.
    - Fall.
    - Redemption.
    - Consummation.
- The authority of the Bible—Jesus received it as God's Word.
- There are practical questions about copies and translations.

Prayer:

- All people pray—but is it prayer that God hears?
- Memorize the Lord's Prayer.
- Use the Lord's Prayer:
    - Pray thinking of a hand: the palm and five fingers.

Assignments

1. **Complete your reading of Mark.** You should have read Mark at least two times before going on to the next part of the study. Are you writing your thoughts and questions in your journal? Don't be surprised that every reading brings new things to light—this is God's Word, and you will never be able to take it all in.

2. **Read Genesis 1–4 and Revelation 21–22.** This is your introduction to the big story of the Bible. Note in your journal how the themes begun in Genesis are completed in Revelation. If you are in a group, this will be an important thing to talk about.

3. **Begin to use the Lord's Prayer in your personal praying.** If you do not know it yet, memorize the Lord's Prayer. Then learn to pray by using the prayer, not just saying the words. You can begin by slowly repeating the prayer and then adding in your own words. Don't forget to touch your hand and fingers as you learn this simple pattern.

PART TWO

DISCIPLESHIP THROUGH THE GOSPEL

You have been introduced to Jesus, the Messiah and the Son of God. This, we have seen, is the *beginning* of the gospel (Mark 1:1). Now it is time to dig more deeply into the gospel. This will be the heart of our study of discipleship—not leaving the gospel behind, but grasping and living out more and more of the gospel. So this part is entitled "Discipleship through the Gospel."

The apostle Paul's letter to the church of Rome suggests four steps in taking disciples deeper into the gospel. Just as you carefully studied Mark in part one, you need to do the same with Romans in part two.

Step One: Know the gospel itself
Chapter 4: The Gospel of God

Step Two: Know how you came to believe the gospel

Chapter 5: The Call to Salvation and Discipleship
Chapter 6: Conversion

Step Three: Know the benefits of believing the gospel (gospel doctrines)

Chapter 7: A New Record: Justification
Chapter 8: A New Life: Sanctification and Adoption
Chapter 9: A New Future: Glorification

Step Four: Live a life that flows from the gospel (gospel obedience)

Chapter 10: Faith Expressing Itself in Love
Chapter 11: The Gospel Changes Everything

STEPS IN THE WALK OF DISCIPLESHIP

- ✗ **Step One: Know the gospel itself**
- Step Two: Know how you came to believe the gospel
- Step Three: Know the benefits of believing the gospel (gospel doctrines)
- Step Four: Live a life that flows from the gospel (gospel obedience)

CHAPTER 4

The Gospel of God

IF YOU HAVE been around Christians and the church very much, you know that the word *gospel* is ordinarily used for the message that pagans or unbelievers need to hear. In one variation or another, it is the good news that Jesus came to forgive our sins by dying on the cross. We can be forgiven by faith in Jesus. A person who believes this message is said to be *saved.* This is all very true, and it is wonderful good news. But is this all the gospel means? This is a key question in any discussion of discipleship because a common pattern among Christians is to believe the gospel in order to *become* a disciple but then to look to something other than the gospel as the means to *grow* as a disciple.

Stop and think about this for a moment. Or talk about it with others in your group. If you fit the category of a renewed disciple, it is particularly important that you take a fresh look at how you understand the gospel. You may need to start over to let the Scripture, and not your traditional understanding, define the gospel. That is why I'm taking a "discipleship for dummies" approach and trying to let the Scripture speak for itself. Reading about the gospel from Mark and now Romans opens a wonderful door into the majesty and power of the gospel.

Let's think about Titus again. He has been meeting with the disciples in Rome for several months. He is fascinated with their study of the gospel from Mark and feels drawn to Jesus. He feels very welcome in the group and can even carry on an intelligent conversation as the stories of Jesus become more familiar. He is still not sure whether he sincerely believes *in* Jesus, and he knows that if he wants to be known as a disciple he must seek out the elders and ask to be baptized. He hasn't taken that step yet. (Have you? We will talk more about your personal following of Jesus in chapter 6.)

Now something new happens. A letter arrives with some disciples traveling to Rome. The letter tells the church that Paul, the apostle, is coming for a visit. But Paul didn't just send a message telling of his plans; the letter itself is a long discussion of the gospel. The church begins to prepare for the visit of Paul by reading and discussing his letter. Titus has even more to think about, and it quickly becomes clear to him that there is no way that he can take in everything that Paul writes about. But the core idea that came through Mark is also in Paul's writing—to be a disciple of Jesus, one must answer his call to repent, believe the gospel, and follow him.

Our Titus, of course, is a fictional character, but the idea of someone like him studying the gospel according to Mark and then the epistle to the Romans is very plausible. We don't know the precise time of their writing, but they were circulating in Rome at about the same time. You will find that Romans is very different from Mark. Both are about the gospel. Mark, however, tells the gospel as a story, and Paul explains the meaning of the gospel in careful detail. Don't expect to immediately understand everything Paul teaches about the gospel, but he wrote to a church of new believers, and if you are a new or renewed disciple, there is a great deal that you can already understand and apply.

Time Out

Who was Paul?

You did not read about Paul in Mark's gospel. He was not one of the original apostles and in fact persecuted the disciples in the early days of the church. At that time his name was Saul, and he was a highly educated scholar and leader living in Jerusalem. On the road from Jerusalem to Damascus, Syria, Jesus met Saul in a vision, and Saul was converted and called to take the gospel to the nations. Jesus made him one of his apostles. Saul's name was changed to *Paul*, and he went on to become the greatest missionary of the early church. Thirteen of the books of the New Testament are letters written by Paul. Learn more about him by reading the New Testament book of Acts, chapters 9–28.

Begin by carefully reading 1:1–17, the introductory verses of Romans. Paul begins by restating the gospel (1:1–5), then greets the church and describes his upcoming trip (1:6–15), and finally sets out the agenda of what will follow—the gospel as a revelation of the righteousness of God (1:16–17). As you read, count or mark each time the word *gospel* appears (some translations use *good news*). After you read, I will ask four questions about the gospel that are answered in the first verses of Romans. It is time to do some Bible study![1]

Read Your Bible: Romans 1:1–17

WHAT IS THE GOSPEL? (1:1–5)

Notice that as soon as Paul identifies himself, he restates the gospel (reread verses 1–4). He calls it "the gospel of God," which can also be read "God's gospel." This is good news from God himself. The gospel:

- Is promised in the Holy Scriptures (the Old Testament).
- Is about God's Son.
- Is about what happened to that Son:
    - He came to earth as a man, born as a descendant of David.
    - He was raised from death by the power of the Holy Spirit.
- Declares that the resurrection of Jesus makes it clear that Jesus Christ is the Son of God and that he is Lord.

In his letter Paul will explain in great detail the implications of the gospel and the blessings that come through the

1. Many of you reading from Bibles that are very free translations or paraphrases may find yourself confused when we try to do careful Bible study and focus on key words. At some point you will want to "graduate" to Bible translations that may not read as easily but will get you closer to the original text.

gospel. But this brief statement of the essence of the gospel is the same as we discovered in Mark—it is the story of Jesus. That story is Jesus the Messiah, the Son of God, who comes to earth announcing the good news of the kingdom—that God has fulfilled his promise to lift the curse of sin and bring salvation to the world. The result of this salvation is peace, which in Hebrew is the familiar word *shalom.* Jesus brought about this salvation by his death and resurrection. Paul will use various expressions to speak of the gospel, such as: "the message of Christ and him crucified" and "Christ died for our sins . . . and that he was raised on the third day" (1 Corinthians 2:2, 15:3–5). But however it is expressed, God's gospel is the gospel about Jesus Christ.

As you read Romans and the rest of Paul's letters, you will notice that every one of them begins with the greeting "Grace and peace." This is very profound. Peace is what everyone seems to be searching for—peace among nations, peace with family and other relationships, peace of mind. It is a common greeting all over the world (in Arabic, for example, *shalom* becomes *salaam*). But where does peace come from? The gospel answer is that it comes from grace. Grace is God's giving freely what we cannot earn or do not deserve. Salvation is by grace, a gift of God, and because of grace we have "peace with God through our Lord Jesus Christ" (Rom. 5:1). Therefore, Paul's greeting is not just "Peace," but "Grace and peace."

Paul's mission, for which he "received grace and apostleship," was to proclaim this good news of Christ's coming and lordship and to call Gentile people to follow Jesus, "to the obedience that comes from faith" (1:5).

Time Out

Who are the Gentiles?

As you read Romans, you will constantly read references to the "Gentiles" (sometimes "Greek" is used). Usually the term is contrasted with "Jews." A Gentile was anyone who was not a Jew. The word also means "nations" and sounds like the English word *ethnic.* God set apart the Jewish people to be his channel of blessing for the whole world. But the Jews forgot that fact and assumed that Jesus and the kingdom were for only them. The first disciples were Jews, and the message that the gospel was also for the Gentiles was hard for them to agree to (read about this in Acts 15). Paul was a Jew, but his particular mission to Gentile nations was a constant reminder that the gospel takes down walls—walls that keep us from God and from others.

WHO WAS GOING TO HEAR THE GOSPEL? (1:6–15)

Paul was writing to all in Rome who were God's beloved and called to be saints (v. 7). In verse 6 he notes that these same people "are among those who are *called* to belong to Jesus Christ." Here is the theme of the call again—just as we saw at the beginning of Jesus' ministry in Mark. (More about *your* call to follow Jesus in chapter 5.)

Read again about Paul's plan to visit them so that he could "preach the gospel also to you who are at Rome" (1:13–15). These were people whose "faith is being reported all over the

Time Out

Meet Jack and Rose Marie Miller.

Dr. C. John (Jack) Miller was a seminary professor, missionary, and pastor whose life and ministry was transformed by the simple idea I've just stated—that the gospel is just as important after you believe it as before. It is not a new idea, but it seems as though almost every generation must rediscover this life-changing truth, and God used Jack Miller to bring it to bear on the generation that ushered in the twenty-first century. Not only did he teach this principle in his classes at Westminster Theological Seminary, but it was demonstrated in the church he founded, New Life Presbyterian Church of Glenside, Pennsylvania, and the mission that carries on his legacy, World Harvest Mission.[1]

One reason for Jack's impact is that he was very real and vulnerable about his struggle with sin. For added insights, you need to meet Jack's wife, Rose Marie, who tells the story of their relationship as well as her struggle to understand and apply the gospel to her own life. Rose Marie tells that story in her book *From Fear to Freedom*.[2] After Jack passed away in 1996, Rose Marie moved to London to serve her Lord by sharing the gospel with Asian women there.

1. Appendix A, "Further Reading," includes several books written by Jack that will encourage and challenge you in your life of discipleship. I especially recommend a book written just before his death, *A Faith Worth Sharing* (Phillipsburg, NJ: P&R Publishing, 1999), in which you meet Jack through his conversations with believers and unbelievers.

2. Colorado Springs: Shaw Books, 1994.

world" (v. 8). In other words, when Paul was thinking of coming to Rome to preach the gospel, it was to the *church* of Rome, to people who had already come to believe the gospel and had declared themselves to be disciples of Jesus.

Here is the point:

- Do you want to become Jesus' disciple? *Repent, believe the gospel*, and *follow Jesus*.
- Do you want to grow stronger as a disciple of Jesus? *Repent, believe the gospel*, and *follow Jesus*.

As I said earlier in this chapter, nothing is more important for our study of discipleship than understanding this concept: whether you are a "seeker," a new disciple, a renewed disciple, or a mature disciple, you need the same message—the gospel of God, the good news of the coming of Jesus to bring salvation.

HOW IS THE GOSPEL THE POWER OF GOD? (1:16)

Take a moment and reread verse 16 carefully. This theme of the power of God (it comes from the Greek root for our words *dynamite* and *dynamic*) is another reminder that discipleship is ultimately a supernatural working of God in the lives of people such as you and I. When Jesus called those first disciples, they followed because the power of God was at work in their souls. This is still true, and according to verse 16, that power is at work in us as we believe the gospel. Paul's expression is that the gospel is "the power of God for the *salvation* of everyone who believes." We will learn in future lessons that this refers to more than the time in your life when you first believe and become a disciple. "Salvation" is the total gift; later in Romans it is described as *calling*, *justification*, and *glorification*—God's graciously giving us *all things* (8:30, 32).

Are you connecting the dots?

- The gospel is God's power in us for *all* our salvation, from our calling to our final glory.
- This power is for everyone who believes the gospel.
- This means that if we are to effectively live out our discipleship, it must be a life lived by believing the gospel—a life in which we learn to trust more and more in Jesus and the wonderful things about him revealed in the gospel.

An important church historian, Richard Lovelace, asked why the church has seemed to live in a pattern of powerlessness until a new awakening or revival brought about renewal. He asked why renewal couldn't be part of the ongoing life of the church and the daily life of every believer. This could happen, he taught, through what he called *a depth presentation of the gospel*, and his writings explained what that could look like.[2] Many churches and ministries have been impacted by this teaching; it is a living example of how believing the gospel will give us power to grow as disciples of Jesus.

For Reflection

Think about this, or talk about it in your group: Doesn't it make sense that the more we grow in our understanding and

2. Richard F. Lovelace, *Dynamics of Spiritual Life: An Evangelical Theology of Renewal* (Downers Grove, IL: InterVarsity Press, 1979). The writing of Dr. Lovelace had a significant impact on Jack Miller and other leaders of the New Life churches as they formed a vision for churches with both gospel outreach and gospel renewal.

embrace of the gospel, the more we will know of the power of God at work in our lives and our churches?

WHAT IS REVEALED IN THE GOSPEL? (1:17)

To complete the lesson about the gospel of God, read verse 17 again. Paul says that in the gospel there is a revelation of the righteousness of God. The NIV translates this concept as "a righteousness *from* God," which conveys the idea that the gospel tells the story of how God, who is righteous, gives his righteousness to us. This is a very important gospel truth, and we will come back and study it in chapter 7. In fact, the theme of righteousness reappears in every part of the letter to the Romans.

In the Bible, God's righteousness is frequently paired with his justice—the righteous God will always act in true justice (see Isa. 32:1, 16–17; 33:5–6). Therefore, tied to the theme of righteousness is that of God the Judge and his judgment. That is *not* good news for us. So we have to ask, *How does the gospel's revealing of God's righteousness to unrighteous people mean good news?* The answer to that question is the theme of Paul's letter.

Look again at the last part of verse 17 to finish this important lesson. The righteousness of (or from) God, revealed in the gospel, is a righteousness *by faith*. It is called faith "from first to last." Literally that reads "*from* faith *to* faith." Then Paul quotes from a prophet of the Old Testament, Habakkuk, to show that finding righteousness through faith is not a new idea. This means that coming to God by faith has always been God's way, and now it has come to fulfillment with the coming of Jesus Christ.

Time Out

What is righteousness? I thought it was a bad thing.

You are probably thinking of *self-righteousness*: people's thinking they are better than others. That is not a good thing. Think about righteousness by starting with the word *right. Right* speaks of the standard by which things are measured. We want to do the *right* thing. We want to be *right* when we get into an argument. So God is righteous because he always does what is right and he declares what is right. One of the ways in which God is perfect is his perfect or pure *righteousness*. When we compare ourselves to God's righteous standard, we are *un*righteous. For an unrighteous person to think of himself or herself as righteous causes the person to be *self*-righteous.

Does this all make sense? Of course not—yet. But isn't a key part of discipleship being a learner? I hope you will be patient and take in what you can. If you hold on to one thing after this study, I hope it will be the lesson that growth as a follower of Jesus doesn't mean somehow graduating from the gospel for some higher teaching. We need to learn how to dig more deeply into this treasure that is called the gospel of God.

Paul ends Romans on the same note with which he begins the letter—the gospel. He closes by saying, "Now to him who is able to establish you *by my gospel*" (16:25). That is my prayer as we continue this study.

Summary of Chapter 4

The most important way to grow as a disciple of Jesus is to dig deeper into the gospel. This is the purpose of Paul's writing his letter to the church of Rome, in addition to telling them about his upcoming visit.

Mark told us the gospel, the story of Jesus; Paul tells the same story but also explains more of what it means.

Read the introductory verses of Romans (1:1–17) to answer four questions:

- What is the gospel?
    - The story of Jesus, his person, and his work.
- Who was going to hear the gospel?
    - The church in Rome.
- How is the gospel the power of God?
    - By believing it, we embrace the supernatural work of God through Christ.
- What is revealed in the gospel?
    - A revelation of the righteousness of God.

Take in what you can. As a disciple, whether new or renewed, you have a great deal to learn, so don't be discouraged that you don't "get it" all at once.

Assignments

1. **Continue to use the Lord's Prayer to learn how to pray.** You might want to read Luke 11:1–13 to note how the first disciples asked for help in learning to pray. Follow

the model of the hand guiding you through the requests. Write about your progress, and talk with others if you are in a group.

2. **Continue to read your Bible regularly.** Read the gospel according to John. You will notice that John tells the gospel story in a way that seems to assume that the disciples have already read Mark. John fills in more information about the ministry of Jesus and gives more of his teaching. Read John as we are working on the next two lessons. If you have time, read Paul's letter to the Galatians as well. You will learn that the Galatian churches had the problem of leaving the gospel, which upset Paul very much.

3. **Write the first draft of your spiritual autobiography.** In the next lesson we return to the matter of God's call on your life. Write down the thoughts you have at this point in our studies about God's working in your life and your response to the call to follow Jesus.

STEPS IN THE WALK OF DISCIPLESHIP

Step One: Know the gospel itself

✗ **Step Two: Know how you came to believe the gospel**

Step Three: Know the benefits of believing the gospel (gospel doctrines)

Step Four: Live a life that flows from the gospel (gospel obedience)

CHAPTER 5

The Call to Salvation and Discipleship

THINK BACK TO the first lesson of this study, about the beginning of the gospel. From Mark we were given a picture of Jesus' calling people to repent, believe the gospel, and follow him. He said that he had not come to call the righteous but sinners. When we began our study of Romans for a deeper understanding of the gospel, Paul started out by reminding the Romans that they had been "called to belong to Jesus Christ"; they were "called to be saints."

Do you begin to see a pattern here? Discipleship begins with a divine call. When we respond to the gospel, we follow—but it is answering the call. This is how I defined *disciple* in the first lesson: "a disciple of Jesus is one who has heard the call of Jesus and has responded by repenting, believing the gospel, and following Jesus." The more I have thought about this idea of God's call, the more I have noticed how often Paul brought up the subject with the churches to which he wrote. I'm convinced he believed that a key element in their growth as disciples was reminding them of where they had been and the greatness of God's love to call them out of darkness into the light of the gospel. It has also become clear to me that the call to discipleship seen in Jesus' preaching is essentially the same as the call to salvation through the preaching of Paul and others. *The call to salvation is the call to discipleship.*

We are going to study more about the call, but this is also an important time for you to reflect on God's work in your life. God is still calling men and women and children to belong to Jesus Christ and follow him as disciples. If the gospel is the story of Jesus, it is now time to consider your own story.

I WAS A TITUS

We started by introducing Titus, a pagan who knew nothing at all about Jesus and the gospel. I have tried to imagine how someone like Titus might react to reading Mark and hearing the gospel for the first time. After reading Mark, he was stretched even more by reading Romans. And all the while, he knew he needed to answer the call and publicly confess Jesus as his Lord and be baptized. How did he respond? Did he lose interest and walk away? Did he go through the motions and "join the church" without being serious about living as a disciple? Or was he deeply changed from a life of unbelief? And from knowing next to nothing, did he slowly grow in faith and live out a life of following Jesus? Of course, we can't know how a fictional Titus responded to the call, but my own story is just like that of Titus, and I can tell the story of how God worked in my life. My story is one variation of a story that can be told by millions of people.

No two of us have identical stories, but when it is the gospel call and we respond, it leads to the same result—we are "called to belong to Jesus Christ" (Rom. 1:6). That is why I assigned you the task of writing the first draft of your spiritual autobiography. You will probably want to revise it as you learn more, but you need to think deeply about God's work in your life.

For Reflection

If you are studying with others, this would be a good time to stop and talk briefly about your own religious and spiritual background if you have not already done this. Are you like Titus, with no background at all? Have you grown up in a nominal Christian setting? Have you had a strong Christian home? What were the first things that made you think more seriously about Jesus?

HOW DOES THE CALL WORK?

In your Bible, find the brief letter called First Thessalonians (Thessalonica was a city in Greece that today is called Thessaloniki). Paul wrote two letters to this young congregation shortly after he was forced to leave them because of an angry mob. (You can read about this episode in Acts 17:1–15.) In both letters he takes time to remind them of how the gospel had worked to change them.

Read Your Bible: 1 Thessalonians 1:4–10

Paul knew that the Thessalonians were God's chosen ones because of what happened when the gospel was preached. By itself the gospel is only words—true and wonderful words, but

Time Out

Tell me more about the Holy Spirit.

From the very start of the Bible, it is clear that God is far more complex than a single being. In the second verse of the Bible we read that "the Spirit of God was hovering over the waters" as God began the work of creation (Gen. 1:2). But the main message of the Old Testament, with all the idolatry that was present in the ancient world, was that God is One. With the coming of Jesus, it is more clearly revealed that the God who is One is more than that—he is Three in One: the Father, the Son, and the Holy Spirit

only words. But in this city, when Paul preached the gospel it came alive to people because of the working of the Holy Spirit. There was power and deep conviction—the gospel moved into their souls, and they were changed. They turned away from idols (repentance) to serve God (following Jesus).

This introduces a new aspect of God's call: the power of the Holy Spirit. How can the gospel call change people? It changes them because the Holy Spirit presses the truth of the gospel into hearts in a way that transforms them from within. The word for this phenomenon (which we will talk about later) is *regeneration*.

In the great work of salvation, each person of the Trinity has a key part. It was planned by the Father, fulfilled by the coming of the Son, and applied to sinners' hearts by the work of the (in older language, the Holy Ghost). When the virgin Mary conceived a child, it was from the Holy Spirit (Matt. 1:20). Do you remember reading in Mark 1 that when Jesus was baptized, the Holy Spirit came upon him and a voice from heaven (who would have been the Father) called him "my Son, whom I love" (Mark 1:12)? The word used by the church to speak of God is *Tri-unity*, or *Trinity*. This is how God reveals himself in the Bible—the great mystery is *revealed* but never *explained*, and we must be cautious before trying to explain it ourselves. The Holy Spirit is the One who works invisibly in the world, accomplishing the purposes of God and pointing the way, not to himself but to Jesus.

Spirit. Notice how clearly these ideas are brought together in the second letter Paul wrote to the Thessalonians:

Read Your Bible: 2 Thessalonians 2:13–15

God works through "the sanctifying work of the Spirit" (2 Thess. 2:13). This means that the Holy Spirit is the One who sets us apart (in the Old Testament, an animal was "sanctified" when it was separated from the herd to be prepared for sacrifice). Notice that this happens when we are called through the gospel. To the church in another Greek city, Corinth, Paul wrote that from a human perspective the gospel made no sense to either Jews or Greeks (Gentiles). But "to those whom God has *called*, both Jews and Greeks, Christ [is] the power of God and the wisdom of God" (1 Cor. 1:24). In other words, when the Spirit moves into people's hearts and minds, the gospel comes alive and we believe in Jesus the Messiah, the Son of God, and follow him. Doesn't this help to explain why those first disciples could hear the call of Jesus and immediately get up and follow? It also helps to explain why individuals can hear exactly the same gospel message and respond very differently.

For Reflection

Stop and think about how your understanding of the gospel began to change. Perhaps that is what is going on right now in this study. If you are a "Titus," this is all new. But for many of you, these are ideas you have heard all your lives. Is God taking those "old" truths and making them come alive? Talk about this if you are part of a group.

THE EFFECTUAL CALL

When I first started to understand this idea of God's call, I was a theological student and came across a phrase that was curious to me. The theology text described *effectual calling*. But that old-fashioned word *effectual* simply means "producing a desired effect." When God calls, we come! The textbook explained that there is a difference between the gospel call and the effectual call. I found that idea helpful because not everyone responds to the call of the gospel. Many will turn away and even become harder. Therefore, it takes the call of the Holy Spirit in our hearts to make the call of the gospel work. In fact, if we think about our own attitudes, we recognize that none of us would respond to the gospel if we were left to ourselves.

When I think about my own situation, I am reminded that the only reason I became interested in the gospel was that I had been invited to join a church basketball team and thought I should show up in church once in a while. I was not on some great spiritual quest—God used something ordinary to get me started. The gospel meant nothing at first, but gradually it made more and more sense, and my need to surrender my life to Christ became more and more pressing. Finally I responded to the gospel call, and as a young man of sixteen I prayed a prayer of surrender. It was the beginning of a new life—and yet it was not the beginning. God had been working in my heart for some time. This was my experience of the effectual call.[1]

Later in my spiritual journey I discovered a wonderful treasure called the Westminster Shorter Catechism. This work is a series of 107 questions and answers that go step by step through the teachings of the Bible.[2] I love the way the catechism explains effectual calling. Take a few minutes and reflect on this:

> *What is effectual calling?*
>
> Effectual calling is the work of God's Spirit, whereby, convincing us of our sin and misery, enlightening our minds in the knowledge of Christ, and renewing our wills, He persuades and enables us to embrace Jesus Christ, freely offered to us in the gospel. (Shorter Catechism no. 31)

1. I tell this story in greater detail in my booklet *What Is True Conversion?* (Phillipsburg, NJ: P&R Publishing, 2006).

2. I encourage you to put a study of the Shorter Catechism on your "to do" list for growth in understanding the faith. P&R publishes the *Westminster Shorter Catechism in Modern English*.

The end result of the effectual calling of the Spirit is that we "embrace Jesus Christ, freely offered to us in the gospel." That is a beautiful way to describe what is often called *conversion*. We will devote the next lesson to this important topic. But at this point it is vital to understand that our embrace of Jesus is a gift to us because of the work of the Holy Spirit. We often celebrate in song and words God's great love in sending his Son into the world, and so we should. But not only has God given his Son to be our Savior, he has given his Spirit to break open our closed hearts and give life to our dead spirits.

Have you given much thought to the work of the Holy Spirit before your conversion? This is a new idea for many, even those who have been believers for some time. It is mysterious but very comforting to realize that long before we were seeking God, he was seeking and calling us. No wonder many speak of how impossible it was to get away from God in spite of their rebellious ways.

Time Out

What happened to "free will"?

That's a great question. Think about it! Is there such a thing as free will? Evolutionary scientific theories and many forms of psychology tell us that our choices are simply the result of our genes or brain chemistry. Maybe a better question is why we always use our "free will" to establish our own autonomy. We want our freedom, no matter what the cost. Even if we claim to believe in God, it is because he exists to meet our needs. So from various points of view, we can reasonably conclude that the idea of having a free will is more myth than reality.

YOU MUST BE BORN AGAIN

Jesus presents the truth of God's effectual call in a very familiar term: *born again.* One of the common expressions used to describe serious Christians is to call them "born again." Does this mean that you can be a Christian and *not* be born again? That is a question to ask Jesus himself. The phrase *born again* comes from an important conversation that Jesus had with a Jewish teacher named Nicodemus.

Read Your Bible: John 3:1–8

Nicodemus seemed shocked by Jesus' statement that he needed to be born again to enter the kingdom and thought immediately of physical birth. I believe that is exactly what Jesus intended because he continued to use the idea of physical birth

> From the point of view of the Bible, we are taught that God created us with a free will, but that as fallen beings we are now in bondage to our passions and selfish desires (remember the big story of creation and fall?). So we seem to have a *memory* in our souls of what it is like to have true freedom, but it is not something we actually experience. The good news is that the call of God breaks the bondage of sin in our lives and that when we turn to "embrace Jesus Christ, freely offered . . . in the gospel" (Shorter Catechism no. 31), it is because we are finally free. Jesus said, "If the Son sets you free, you will be free indeed" (John 8:36).

to explain spiritual birth. *Born again* can also mean "born from above" or even "begotten from above." It refers to a work that the Holy Spirit does in the human spirit ("the Spirit gives birth to spirit," v. 6). And Jesus is quite emphatic that a person must be born of the Spirit to enter the kingdom of God. This must happen (v. 7), but it is not something that Nicodemus could do or that any of us can do—it is what the Spirit must do in us.

And this concept is mysterious, like the blowing of the wind (v. 8). How can any of us truly understand the moving of God in the human soul? We do know the outcome: the moving of the Spirit brings us to the place of faith in Jesus Christ the Son of God. That is what Jesus tells Nicodemus later in the conversation: "For God so loved the world that he gave his one and only Son, that whoever believes in him shall not perish but have eternal life" (3:16).

I have been describing what theologians call *regeneration*. It is an important word, and you should understand that it means the work of the Holy Spirit generating new life in one who is spiritually dead (so it is *re*generating life). It is another word for the new birth. In a letter to Titus (a real Titus, not the Titus of this book), Paul called this idea "the washing of rebirth and renewal by the Holy Spirit" (Titus 3:5).

Several years ago I drew out the picture of physical and spiritual birth on a timeline. We now call this the *spiritual birthline*.[3] Take a few minutes to study the diagram on the next page comparing the two births.

The top part of the diagram is the process of physical birth, beginning with conception when the new life grows until the time of actual delivery. After the "birthday," the newborn baby

3. This idea is explained in detail in my book *Spiritual Birthline: Understanding How We Experience the New Birth* (Wheaton, IL: Crossway Books, 2006).

Fig. 3. Physical/Spiritual birthline

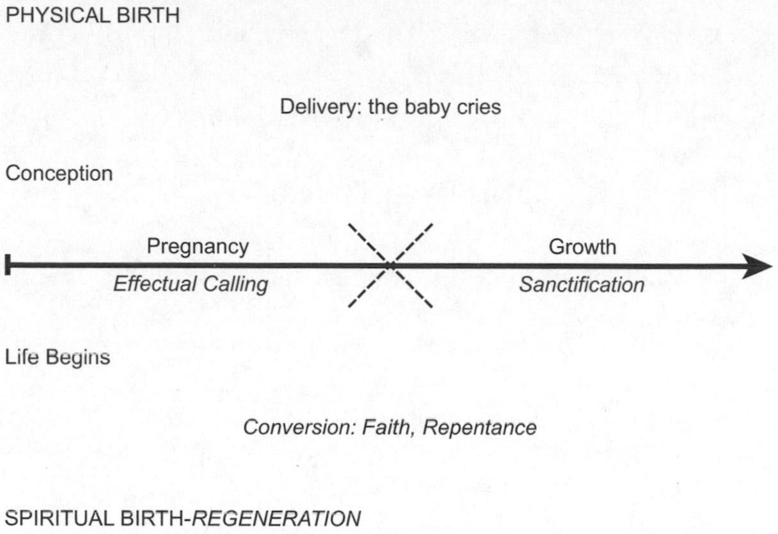

keeps growing, but now it is breathing and eating on its own. The mystery of God's work of regeneration follows a similar pattern. The key is to remember that the time when we cry out, in prayer or confession (conversion), is a result of what God has been doing through the effectual call. People often think of their conversion as the beginning of their spiritual lives. But the birthline diagram is a reminder that new birth is really a process, with conversion as a response to the call of God. Many people have found this to be a helpful way to understand their own calling to salvation as well as how God's Spirit works in others.

For Reflection

Give more thought to what God's effectual call was (or is) like in your own life. Write about this or talk about it in your group. Can you describe your journey in terms of the spiritual birthline? Have you passed the point of that X on the diagram? If not, do you have the sense that the Holy Spirit is pushing you toward becoming a disciple of Jesus?

Summary of Chapter 5

The call to salvation is the call to discipleship. It is time to think deeply about God's call to you.

How does the call work?

- The gospel call goes out.
- The Holy Spirit gives life to the words of the gospel.
- Those who are called find power and wisdom in Jesus.

The effectual call:

- When God calls, we come!
- "What is effectual calling?" (Shorter Catechism no. 31)

You must be born again:

- Jesus' explanation of regeneration: birth through the Holy Spirit.
- The spiritual birthline, comparing physical and spiritual birth.

Assignments

1. **Continue reading your Bible regularly.** Finish reading John. The book was written to help you believe in Jesus as the Son of God. It will fill in the picture of Jesus that you got from reading Mark. If you have time, also read Paul's

letter to the Colossians. This is a short letter that builds on the gospel to point to the sufficiency of Christ. In Christ you have all you need.

2. **Continue learning to pray by using the Lord's Prayer.** Are you learning to take time in your day or week to be quiet in God's presence? This is a time to read, pray, write in your journal, and think about the lessons you are learning about being Jesus' disciple.

3. **Ask someone about his or her spiritual journey.** Keep in mind the concept of the spiritual birthline—that coming to faith is more a journey than an event. Ask someone who is not in your study group—perhaps someone else at your church, or at work or in your family. Tell that person about what you have been learning and then ask about his or her background and what the person is thinking now. Pray first about the right person to talk to. The key here is that you are trying to learn how to listen respectfully.

CHAPTER 6

Conversion

THE GREAT STORY of conversion in the New Testament is Saul's meeting Jesus on the road from Jerusalem to Damascus. He was knocked off his horse and heard Jesus call his name. At that moment his life was turned around, and he began to follow the very Jesus whom he had been fighting against. The change was so radical that even his name was changed, and we know him as the apostle Paul. It is a wonderful true story. But should it be the model for all conversions to Christ, as many assume? What about the millions who have been converted since then but did not have the same experience?

A REVIEW

Think back to the first lesson when we studied the "beginning of the gospel" in Mark 1. We were introduced to Jesus, the Messiah and the Son of God. But before we learned much more about Jesus, we were challenged by him to repent, believe the gospel, and follow. Therefore, included in the gospel from the beginning is the expectation that we must respond to the call of the gospel. We have now come to understand that the ability to respond comes from the power of the Holy Spirit in our effectual calling. So God is working, but his work is to "persuade and enable us to embrace Jesus Christ, freely offered to us in the gospel" (Shorter Catechism no. 31). Because the Spirit works, we respond. In the first lesson I explained that the response of repenting, believing the gospel, and following Jesus is another way to speak of *conversion*.

The basic idea of conversion is to change or turn. We must embrace Jesus freely offered in the gospel, but to do that, we must turn to a new direction. Jesus is not on the path we walk as sinners. As I said in our first lesson, we cannot *add* Jesus to our lives; we must *turn* to him. This is conversion.

To explain conversion, I pictured two walls facing each other. One wall represents the path without God. For some, that may mean a very crude and evil life with destructive behavior that harms self and others. But that path may represent a "good" life, one of caring and family and even a hint of religion or spirituality. Nevertheless, it is still a life that revolves around one's own needs and fulfillment. The opposite wall represents Jesus and the forgiveness of sins and eternal life that he gives. The call of the gospel comes from that direction. To respond to and believe in the gospel, we must turn—this is *repentance*. As we turn, our arms reach out by *faith* to embrace Jesus.

Fig. 4. Conversion, repentance, and faith

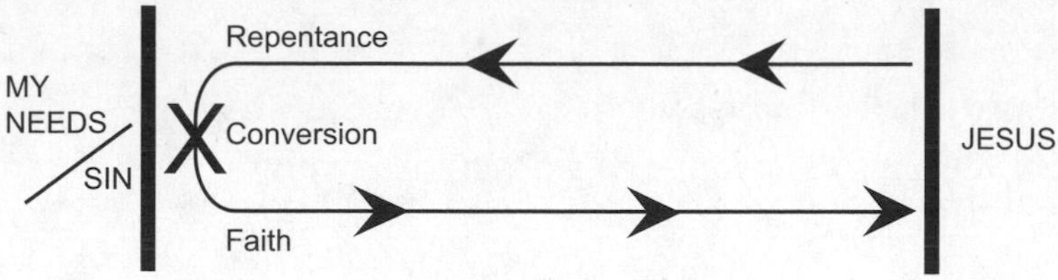

CONVERSION EXPERIENCES

Repentance and faith are the two basic elements of conversion. That is an easy concept to diagram, but it is not as easy in terms of actual experiences. Look again at the birthline diagram in the last lesson (p. 93). Notice that I represent conversion by making an X through the timeline. Just like a baby who is conceived and grows to the point of delivery when the newborn cries out, so the work of the Holy Spirit will bring those he is effectually calling to the place of conversion and into a new life with Christ.

If you look at the X carefully, however, you will also notice that it is drawn with a dotted line. That represents the fact that while conversion to Christ is necessary, the experience of conversion will not look the same for everyone. I have learned this truth by asking many people, who were genuinely trusting only in Christ, to describe the actual point of converting from self to Christ. Some have had the experience, just like many babies when they are born, of crying out with grief for sin and desire for Jesus and his salvation. They can even tell you the day and perhaps the hour of their conversion. These are wonderful and often dramatic stories, like that of the conversion of Paul. But when these kinds of conversion stories are the only ones we hear, it is easy to get the impression that all conversions are dramatic moments. "When were you saved?" is a question frequently asked by church people, and often they expect to hear about a specific experience.

However, others are converted through a series of experiences or perhaps no experience at all. I have seen many slowly drawn to Christ, and when they think about it, they cannot point to a clear moment of turning. Many cannot describe praying the "sinner's prayer" for salvation, but they know they have been changed. People have been helped to understand this concept when I draw that diagram of the two walls but make the turning from one wall to the other a very wide turn. In some settings I will actually walk around the room or pulpit area, explaining the convicting work of the Spirit as I gradually turn from facing one wall to the other. It takes a few moments to realize what I am doing, but then people see that I am walking in the opposite direction from where I started. Turning from sin to Christ is a genuine conversion, but with the wide turn it is very difficult to describe *when* the turn took place. But many have told me that this fits their experience of conversion.

The point of this is a reminder that a true conversion to Christ is not defined by a particular kind of experience. If you are not sure that you are converted, you should not be looking for an experience—you need to be looking to Jesus and praying for faith to trust in him alone. In fact, an experience, by itself, can be merely an emotional or human experience. There are far too many examples of people who have made

Fig. 5. Conversion through a slow process

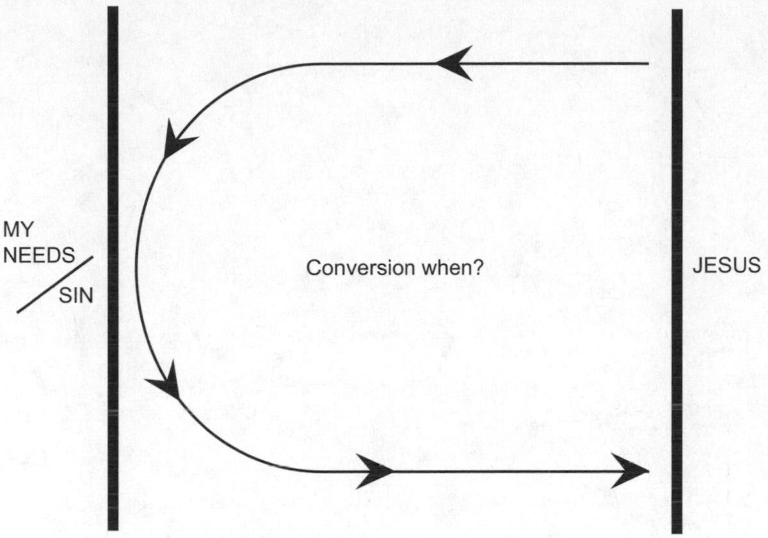

some sort of mental "commitment" but who know nothing of the transforming work of the Spirit. This is not true conversion to Christ.

For most of the disciples of the early church, the defining "moment" was their public confession of faith and baptism. This is still true for places where the gospel is just beginning to be established. But even in places such as the United States, where baptism can be just a formality, it is very important to make a public confession of your faith, even if you were baptized earlier in your life. Paul said to the Romans, "For it is with your heart that you believe and are justified, and it is with your mouth that you confess and are saved" (Rom. 10:10). God knows our hearts, but we must speak of what is in our hearts to help ourselves and others grow in the faith.

Time Out

Some of us come from families that were already following Jesus. Do we need to be converted, too?

When disciples of Jesus marry, they are to marry other disciples. This means that they form a family that is following Jesus. When God gives them children, those children are raised in the "training and instruction of the Lord" (Eph. 6:4). So how do those children repent and believe the gospel when that is how they were raised? Some of you reading this are struggling with that question for yourself or your children. The answer to the question is, "Yes, children raised up as disciples of Jesus must be converted"—but the *experience* of conversion will not necessarily fit the pattern of others. You must repent of sin and believe the gospel, but this may be something that comes very naturally to you because of your family. The challenge again is not to focus on a particular kind of experience but the direction in which your life is headed.[1]

1. Chapter 13 of my book *Spiritual Birthline: Understanding How We Experience the New Birth* (Wheaton, IL: Crossway Books, 2006) goes into more detail about the conversion of children from Christian families. In it I relate the spiritual journeys of my four children. I also have a booklet on this topic: *How Our Children Come to Faith* (Phillipsburg, NJ: P&R Publishing, 2006).

THE TEST OF TRUE CONVERSION—FOLLOWING JESUS

The call of Jesus clearly includes "follow me." Yet this should not be thought of as a third step we take—after we believe, then we follow.

Following Jesus as his disciple is the normal response of believing the gospel. When we turn, it is not to make a "decision for Jesus," as though we were casting a vote. We turn to follow Jesus—this is a new life, a new path. I hope this discussion makes it clear that from the viewpoint of the Bible, a believer in Jesus is a follower of Jesus. If you are converted, this means that you are a disciple; if you are not a disciple, you are not a believer. Of course, you must grow as a disciple, and there is so much more to learn about this one whom you are following. There will be times of discouragement and doubt and even suffering. Nevertheless, the person converted to Christ will follow him—not just *should* follow him, but *will* follow him.

ARE YOU CONVERTED?

This is an important place to stop and thoughtfully answer the question, "Am I a converted person?" There are several possible answers. You still may not be able to say, "Yes, I am" with certainty, even though you know you *want* to be converted. Try not to question whether or not you are converted based on feeling that you have attained some level of accomplishment as a disciple. You *can* say, "Yes, I believe I am converted," if that means you are trusting in Jesus for your salvation and are *seeking* to follow him. For many of us it takes time as a follower of Jesus before we can look back and know that there was a real turning point. This is another way your participation in the community of believers is crucial—we confess our faith and our sin and our needs to one another, and we pray for one another and seek to follow Jesus together.

You can also answer the question, "No." That can mean, "No, I am not *yet* ready to follow Jesus," or it can mean, "No, I now know that this is not something I want to do. I'm glad

I had a chance to think about this, but I'm not going to be a follower of Jesus." If you walk away, know that Jesus loves you but that he will let you go your way.

Read Your Bible: Mark 10:17–27

This passage is called the story of the "rich young man." He was a man who was face to face with Jesus and heard the call "Follow me," but he went away. I have often wondered how that story ended. I can't imagine that anything would ever look the same after tasting the love of Jesus as that young man did. What do you think? I picture him coming back to Jesus and falling down in total surrender to him. Of course, the Bible doesn't tell us that; it records only that he walked away—that he was sad, but that in the end his "stuff" was more valuable than Jesus.

The disciples were shocked as they watched the man walk away. And they were right when they asked Jesus, "Who then can be saved?" (v. 26), because if it is not riches, then it will be something else that will be keeping us from Jesus. So the final answer is that God himself must change us in order for us to turn and be truly converted.

REGENERATION AND CONVERSION

When Jesus said to the disciples, "With man this is impossible, but not with God" (Mark 10:27), he was talking about the impossibility of man's finding salvation or being truly converted by his own effort. You know how true this is by examining your own heart and your determination to go your own way. But you also know this truth from our study of effectual calling and regeneration. God does the impossible: he gives spiritual life to those who are dead. One picture of regeneration is birth. Jesus taught about being born again, or born of the Spirit, as we saw in John 3. Now read about another picture of regeneration that Paul used in his teaching: resurrection from death.

Read Your Bible: Ephesians 2:1–10

In Ephesians 1:19 Paul prays that we would know the power that is ours in Christ. He then explains that the same power that raised Jesus from the dead also raised us from our death in transgressions and sins (2:1–4). Can you believe that? God has raised us from the dead and made us "alive with Christ" (v. 5) by the same power that raised up Jesus. Why would God do such an amazing thing? The answer this passage gives is that it was done "by grace" (v. 5) by God, "who is rich in mercy" (v. 4). In other words, nothing about us deserves this gift of new life, a gift that is intended to display God's glorious grace in the coming ages (v. 7).

Notice carefully how our salvation is described in these verses because it will open the way to our next lessons. We have been saved by grace, through faith (2:8). It is not faith that saves us but grace (God's work), and we respond to that grace by faith (we believe what God has told us). And even faith is not from ourselves; "it is the gift of God" (v. 8). None of our salvation is by works, and none of us can ever boast that we played even a small part (v. 9).

Ephesians 2:8–9 is a famous text in the teaching of salvation by grace through faith. Unfortunately, many do not read the full thought, which ends in verse 10. That verse teaches us that not only is the beginning of our salvation (a new creation, which is another picture of regeneration) the work of God, but those he saves are "created in Christ Jesus to do good works." The new life we have been given leads to a new purpose in life—we are following Jesus into a life of service for the glory of God.

FAITH AND REPENTANCE

If the fruit of regeneration and conversion could be summed up in a single word, it would be *faith*. Perhaps a better term would be *repentant faith*. That means that repentance and faith will continue as a pattern of our following Jesus as his disciples. Jack Miller wrote, "But what is true of the first turning (conversion) of the sinner to the Lord must continue throughout the Christian life. There must be a daily conversion of the heart to God (Col. 2:6). And the more you deepen your repentance, the more room you have in your heart for the rivers of living water."[1] In the first of his Ninety-five Theses, Martin Luther said, "Our Lord and Master Jesus Christ . . . willed the entire life of believers to be one of repentance."[2]

In chapter 4 we began to look at Paul's letter to the church at Rome to discover more about the gospel. But Paul wrote that letter to teach the gospel to those who already believed it. They were people with faith in Jesus Christ as Lord. Therefore, we have taken some time to study how people come to have such faith. I hope this has helped you to understand on a deeper level how you have come to faith.

1. Jack Miller, *Repentance* (CLC Publications: Fort Washington, PA), 47.

2. Quoted from a brief and very helpful article by Dr. Tim Keller entitled "All of Life Is Repentance." http://download.redeemer.com/pdf/learn/resources/All_of_Life_Is_Repentance-Keller.pdf.

Now it is time to study where that faith takes us. We particularly need to understand the phrase "a righteousness that is by faith" (Rom. 1:17).

Summary of Chapter 6

The conversion of Saul was a dramatic event, but not all conversions look like his.

Review the teaching of Jesus about conversion:

- We must repent and believe the gospel—we must respond to Jesus' call.
- There is a turning from sin to embrace Jesus—repentance and faith.

But conversion does not mean the same experience for all:

- The X on the spiritual birthline is a dotted line.
- Don't judge your conversion by an experience.

The test of true conversion—following Jesus:

- Discipleship doesn't come after believing; it is the same as believing.
- A believer in Jesus follows Jesus, even when it is difficult.

Are you converted? This is an important time for asking a hard question.

Regeneration and conversion:

- God is the One who must change the heart.
- God, who raised Jesus from the dead, raises us from our death in sin.

Faith and repentance:

- The result of regeneration and conversion is faith.
- It could be called *repentant faith* because the pattern of repentance and faith will continue as we follow Jesus.
- We now need to understand the meaning of *faith* in Romans.

Assignments

1. **Rewrite your spiritual autobiography.** What have you learned about your own conversion from these studies? Try to focus on what God was doing to prepare you for believing the gospel rather than on your experiences. Try to interpret your actual conversion—remember, this may not mean describing a particular experience. What have you learned from talking to others about their journeys?

2. **Continue to read your Bible regularly.** Prepare for the next lesson by a careful reading of Romans 1–5. Notice how often Paul quotes Old Testament passages. In the NIV translation, the origins of these quotations are given in footnotes. You should try to trace them back to the Old Testament and read them in that setting. Try also to read some psalms. The book of Psalms is the hymnbook of the Bible and is filled with different kinds of songs and poems that help express our feelings to God.

3. **Continue to pray and keep a journal.** Are you still using the Lord's Prayer? This is a form of praying that will always be helpful, but you may also find that other guides are

helpful. God wants our hearts, not a certain form. Are you praying with others? If you are married, are you learning to pray with your spouse? And with your family? A key part of discipleship is leading our families to follow Jesus.

4. **Have you made a public profession of faith and joined with a community of believers in a local church?** I hope our studies have brought you to this place if you have not yet made this commitment. To whom can you speak to take this important step? You will flounder as a disciple without others to support you and with whom you can serve.

STEPS IN THE WALK OF DISCIPLESHIP

Step One: Know the gospel itself

Step Two: Know how you came to believe the gospel

✗ **Step Three: Know the benefits of believing the gospel (gospel doctrines)**

Step Four: Live a life that flows from the gospel (gospel obedience)

CHAPTER 7

A New Record: Justification

WHEN I TEACH on the topic of the gospel, I often begin by asking people how much of the gospel they understood at the time of their conversion or first coming to a serious awakening of faith. That question usually produces smiles, and we have a good discussion about how *little* people understood about what God had done for them.

How would you answer that question? Of course, the answer will be different for each one of you, depending on your background. If you are a new disciple like Titus, there is a great deal to learn. If you are a renewed disciple, you will have a better background, but you still must be sure that you are on a solid foundation. You may discover that things you have believed need to be corrected. Or have you followed the typical pattern of moving from the gospel of Jesus Christ to the gospel of self-effort and rule-keeping?[1] One of the reasons

1. Paul wrote his epistle to the Galatians to try to correct this problem. God has used the study of Galatians over and over to bring his church back to the gospel.

why disciples "run out of gas" and get discouraged is that they are trying to serve Jesus without appreciating what he has done for them. This brings us to Step Three in Discipleship through the Gospel, the topic that takes up most of Romans. Notice how one step leads to the next:

- **Step One** is to know the gospel story. We must stay centered on Jesus himself, the Messiah and Son of God. Mark and the other three Gospels (Matthew, Luke, and John) were written to introduce "seekers" and new believers to Jesus.[2] Our faith is rooted in a man who actually lived and died and rose again. *The gospel is a true story.*

- **Step Two** is to understand how we personally were called by the power of the Holy Spirit to believe the gospel. The story of the gospel is true, but it is also a story that will change our lives forever. *The gospel is the power of God for the salvation of those who believe.*

- **Step Three** is to go deeper into the gospel as it reveals the righteousness that God has given us in Christ. We can believe the gospel without understanding all the benefits we have been given in Christ, but we will be weak and struggling until we grasp them by faith. That is why Paul wrote Romans. *The gospel reveals a righteousness from God that is ours through faith.*

2. Appendix B is a series of readings in the four Gospels and Acts that will give you a sense of the life and ministry of Jesus. Use them to meditate on the life of Jesus. They are brief enough readings that you can use them to read aloud to your family.

- **Step Four** is the obedience that grows out of faith. The power of the gospel to change the believer shows itself in a different life. We are now on a path that directs us to love God, love our neighbors, and love our fellow believers. *The gospel changes everything.*

CHEER UP—YOU'RE WORSE THAN YOU THINK

Jack Miller, whom you met in chapter 4, would begin to talk about how much believers as well as unbelievers need the gospel because we are all sinners. Then he would pause and with a twinkle in his eye say, "But cheer up—you're worse than you think!" He was right. You and I don't have a clue as to how sinful we really are. That is the *bad news* that Paul emphasizes as we come back to the study of Romans.

Find Romans in your Bible and read 1:17 again, which is the key verse of the book. It teaches that the gospel reveals a righteousness from God—a righteousness that is by faith. Recall that this is where we ended chapter 4, asking how the gospel, revealing God's righteousness, could be good news for those who are *un*righteous. Before he answers the question, Paul makes sure that we understand how unrighteous we are—we really are worse than we think.

Read Your Bible: Romans 1:18–32; 3:9–20.

Notice that like 1:17, 1:18 speaks of something revealed. In verse 18 it is "the wrath of God" revealed against "the godlessness and wickedness of men" (men and women, of course) who should know better because they still have some sense of

God (1:19–21) and something of a conscience (2:14–15). We often focus on the *wickedness* (that word can also be translated *unrighteousness*, which is its literal meaning) of the human race because it is more visible in things such as violence and sexual perversion; but the root of wickedness is *godlessness*. When we move away from God and his law, it will corrupt people and societies.

Time Out

Is this what they call "original sin"?

Yes and no. The Bible teaches that we are born with a determination to sin, coming from the rebellion of Adam and Eve. (This is the part of the big story of the Bible concerning the fall.) It is common to ridicule this idea, but then no one seems to be able to explain why people invariably do the wrong thing. So you usually hear the mention of our "dark side," or people point to villains such as Adolf Hitler and Osama bin Laden to prove that they are not as bad as others. The word sin seems to be radioactive—no one wants to touch it. But the Bible is clear: we sin because at the root of our natures we are sinners. So yes, there is original sin. Children are born rebels, as any of us who are parents know. Sin is part of who we are, but at the same time we sin because we choose to sin. We can't insist on our "free will" and then blame Adam or our genes or our bad background. We are human beings, made in God's image, and in the end we must accept responsibility for what we have done in thought, word, and deed. We will give an accounting to God for choices we have made.

It would be very easy for the people who tried to keep the rules (the Ten Commandments) to agree with Paul as he described the degraded culture of the ancient world. Therefore, starting with 2:1, he also turns his attention to the "good" people who were from a Jewish background ("church" people could fit here, too). He quotes from their Bible (the Old Testament) again and again to point out that "there is no one righteous, *not even one*" (3:10, quoting Ps. 14:1). The bottom line: that every mouth, Jew and Gentile (whether knowing right and wrong from conscience or the Ten Commandments), may be closed and all people understand that we are unacceptable to a perfectly righteous God (3:19). We all deserve his wrath.

BUT NOW A RIGHTEOUSNESS FROM GOD HAS BEEN MADE KNOWN

The bad news of our unrighteousness leads to the good news. Romans 3:21 starts with "But now," marking a big change as Paul begins to explain how a righteous God can receive unrighteous people. The righteousness we lack is found in the Righteous One—Jesus Christ.

Read Your Bible: Romans 3:21–26

You already know about the death of Jesus from your reading of Mark. But why did he die? Perhaps you have a general sense that "Jesus died for me," or "Jesus died for my sins." These important verses explain precisely what such a declaration means. Paul writes of the "redemption that came by Christ Jesus" (v. 24).

Time Out

Why all this talk of blood and sacrifice and wrath? Didn't we leave all that behind in the Dark Ages?

The first way to answer that important question is to ask whether it is based on a proper interpretation of what Paul wrote. We need to base our convictions on the teaching of the Bible, not on what appeals to us. In fact, this teaching is consistent with all the other writings of Paul and the other inspired authors of Scripture. Jesus understood his death to be a ransom (Mark 10:45), the price paid for redemption. The second thing to say is that we must ask ourselves how seriously we view the

Redemption means "rescue through the payment of a price." The price of sin is judgment from God and death, but the one who received that judgment was Jesus, who never sinned. He was a sacrifice, and therefore his blood was shed, just like that of the Old Testament sacrifices. The word for "sacrifice of atonement" (v. 25, if you are reading the NIV) is an old word, *propitiation*, which means "to turn aside wrath" (see NIV footnote). This means that the wrath of God revealed against "all the godlessness and wickedness of men" (Rom. 1:18) was poured out on Jesus! No wonder he cried out on the cross, "My God, my God, why have you forsaken me?" (Mark 15:34). The awful physical pain that Jesus was suffering would have been nothing compared to the agony of knowing that he was separated from God. Notice that he didn't even call him "Father" at that terrible moment.[3]

3. This is one way to understand the phrase "He descended into hell" in the Apostles' Creed. Jesus was in hell as he experienced God's wrath on the cross.

terrible character of sin. We see how destructive it is in our own lives and in the world around us. But how must it offend a righteous God? Seeing sin from that point of view, as we do in Romans 1–3, means that something very radical must happen to deal with sin. Third, the need to somehow atone or pay for sin and wrong is still very much with us. In our hearts we know that evil and injustice cannot go unpunished. People go to extraordinary lengths to relieve an inner sense of guilt in both primitive and sophisticated ways. The gospel doesn't deny that reality, but it points to Jesus as the sacrifice, "the Lamb of God, who takes away the sin of the world" (John 1:29; see also Rev. 5).

The passage goes on to explain that God doesn't stop being a God of perfect justice. God is, at the same time, "just and the one who justifies" (Rom. 3:26) because Jesus, the sinless One, died to bear the penalty for sin—but our sin, not his.

JUSTIFIED FREELY THROUGH FAITH

The language of justice and righteousness comes together in the words *justify* and *justification*. Justice has been done in the death of Jesus, and those who believe in him are "*justified* freely by his grace" (Rom. 3:24). God is the one who "*justifies* [those who have] faith in Jesus" (v. 26). The contrast is between efforts to justify ourselves, by works or keeping God's law (vv. 20, 27–31), and being justified by faith in Jesus Christ. Verse 20 in the NIV reads, "No one will be declared righteous in his sight." "Declared righteous" is another translation of "justified." Go back and read 3:24 and 26 and substitute "declared [or *declares*] righteous" for "justified [or *justifies*]," and this truth will become clearer.

Time Out

Meet Martin Luther.

Martin Luther was a scholar and monk who lived in Germany in the 1500s. Luther was assigned the task of teaching Romans to university students. When he came to Romans 1:17, he was thrown into despair because he read that even the gospel revealed the justice and righteousness of God. He was terrified of God because no matter how hard he tried to obey, he knew that he was still far from the righteousness that God required of him. And if even the gospel revealed the righteousness of God, there was no place left to turn.

As he prepared his lectures, however, Luther began to understand what we have just studied—that the righteousness required by God is found in Jesus, whose death satisfied the justice of God. By faith Luther trusted his standing before God to Jesus instead of his own futile efforts to please God. Luther was so transformed by finally understanding justification that he couldn't hold back from telling this good news. Students flocked to his lectures from Romans. Before long, Luther asked to have a public discussion of these new insights. On October 31, 1517, he nailed to the church door a list of ninety-five propositions, or *theses*, that he wanted discussed. That date is usually used as the beginning of the Protestant Reformation because of what happened as a result of posting the Ninety-five Theses.

Justification is God's declaring us righteous, not because we are righteous but because Jesus is righteous and we have faith in Jesus. Read that sentence over several times, and talk about it if you are part of a group. This is very, very important. Your justification is the reason you can stand before a righteous God. This is a gift that we receive by faith. That means that we simply believe what we have read in these verses—that the death of Jesus Christ the Son of God satisfied the judgment due to us for our sin. This wonderful teaching has been taught in the church as *justification by faith alone.*

FORGIVEN AND COUNTED RIGHTEOUS

Justification gives two amazing blessings to the person who believes in Jesus. First of all, there is forgiveness of sin; and second, a person is actually counted as righteous in the sight of God.

Forgiveness of sin means that the ways in which we have offended God, including our sinful nature, are forgiven. The debt is paid in full. It is all "wiped off the books," so to speak, and there is no longer a record of our sin. We are forgiven, not only because God is loving and merciful, but also because the penalty for our sin has actually been paid. Even when we confess to God the sin that we continue to engage in, our appeal is to what Christ has done for us in his death on the cross.

Most people understand the gift of the forgiveness of sin, but they often miss the other part of justification. *Counted righteous* means that by placing our faith in Jesus, we are actually accepted by God as righteous. The terms used are that we are *declared* righteous, or *counted* as righteous, or that righteousness is *reckoned* to us. The point is that God justifies us even when we are sinners. This is not talking about what we must do to become righteous, but about God's declaring us righteous because Christ is righteous. Sometimes in discussions about justification, you will read the old term that righteousness is *imputed* to us, which means that a characteristic of one is ascribed to someone else. This concept may be hard to take in, but as you read on in Romans 3–5, the idea is reinforced over and over.

Romans 4 explains that justification by faith is not something new. Both Abraham and David were justified by faith. Look at 4:3 and note the language: "Abraham believed God, and it was *credited* to him as righteousness." Paul says that David teaches the same thing (4:6).

Think about our sin as drowning in credit card debt, which grows every day so that it is impossible to pay off. Even if we tried, the growing interest on the debt is much larger than the little bit we put in toward "paying off" the debt. The concept of justification teaches that not only does God pay off that debt (forgiveness of sin), he also applies the infinite credit of Christ's righteousness to our account. Even future sin is covered by the righteousness of Christ.

The Westminster Shorter Catechism, which we studied to understand effectual calling, goes on to describe the *benefits* that come in this life to those who are effectually called. The benefits are justification, adoption, and sanctification.[4]

Here is the catechism's answer to the question "What is justification?":

> Justification is an act of God's free grace, wherein he pardons all our sins, and accepts us as righteous in his sight, only for

4. Shorter Catechism no. 32.

the righteousness of Christ imputed to us, and received by faith alone. (Shorter Catechism no. 33)

A PLACE TO STAND

Think of your justification by faith as bedrock. If you stand on this foundation, nothing can shake you. In Romans 5 Paul explains that since we have been justified by faith, we now have peace *with* God. This is not just the peace *of* God; it means we are no longer enemies. We were in rebellion, but now we are at peace. In 8:1 he states that "there is now no condemnation for those who are in Christ Jesus." This is our place to stand, and when suffering or storms come (as they will), we can still rejoice because through the power of the Holy Spirit the love of God has been poured out to us. That was the second point in Jack Miller's "cheer up" sermons: "Cheer up—God's love is greater than you ever imagined!"

Finish this very important chapter by reading Romans 5:1–11 thoughtfully and prayerfully. Do you get the sense that you are just beginning to appreciate the unimaginable blessings given to you through the gospel? Cheer up! There is much more to come.

Read Your Bible: Romans 5:1–11

Summary of Chapter 7

A review of the four steps of discipleship through the gospel:

- The gospel is a true story.

- The gospel is the power of God for those who believe it.
- The gospel reveals a righteousness from God that is ours by faith.
- The gospel changes everything.

Cheer up—you are worse than you think! This is the bad news from Romans.

But now a righteousness from God has been made known:

- The good news is that the righteousness we need is found in Jesus Christ.
    - Redemption through his blood.
    - Propitiation.
    - God is both just and the One who justifies.

Justified through faith:

- *Justified* means to be declared righteous by God.

Two blessings of justification:

- Forgiveness of sin.
- Counted as righteous.

A place to stand:

- This is bedrock for our faith.

Assignments

1. **Continue to read your Bible regularly.** To prepare for the next lesson, reread Romans 1–5 and then go on to 6–8.

2. **Continue using the Lord's Prayer to learn to pray.**

3. **Review your journal and lessons.** This is a good point to stop and think prayerfully about what you have come to understand about discipleship. The gospel calls for us to respond. Do you see some things you need to be doing to respond to the call of Jesus?

CHAPTER 8

A New Life: Sanctification and Adoption

"WHAT SHALL WE SAY, then? Shall we go on sinning so that grace may increase?" (Rom. 6:1).

That's a great question after our study of justification. If God, by his grace, declares us righteous, even though we aren't, why not just keep on sinning? In fact, the more we sin, the more the grace of God is in evidence. Right? Think about it!

When I come to this part of the study of Romans, I like to answer the question by posing something of a riddle. My statement is, "Yes, because we are justified we are free to do whatever we want." What is the catch in that statement? When I talk about this with a group, it takes a little discussion, but then more and more people see the point. The catch is my use of the word *want*: "we are free to do whatever we *want*." True enough, but as we come to understand the power of the gospel, we realize that what we want has been changed.

Turn to Romans 6 and notice how Paul answers his question in verse 2: "We died to sin; how can we live in it any longer?" As we will see in our reading, Paul now begins to explain the benefit to the believer of the *resurrection*. If we died with Christ, then we have also been raised with him to new life.

We are ready to study the next section of Romans, beginning with chapter 6. This is usually described as the teaching of *sanctification*, even though Paul uses the word only once in these chapters. Think back to the spiritual birthline diagram (p. 93). Using that concept, sanctification can be understood as the growth that follows conversion, similar to the newborn baby growing up. Effectual calling and sanctification are both aspects of the inward and mysterious moving of the Holy Spirit in our souls.

Read Your Bible: Romans 6:1–14

It is important to notice from the reading that Paul is describing what a believer experiences *in the present* by being united to the risen Christ. He means that just as Christ was given new life at his resurrection, so "we too may live a new life" (v. 4). The phrase reads literally "walk in newness of life." In verses 5 and 8 Paul says that we *will* live with him, but he means that this is definitely true, not that it will happen in the future. (There is future resurrection, but that is not what Paul is explaining here.) Look again at verses 10 and 11. Just as Jesus died and is now alive, so we should "count [ourselves] dead to sin but alive to God in Christ Jesus."

Why is this concept so important? It is important because Paul wants to make it clear that living the new life of discipleship is much more than a call to do our part because God did his part in our justification. Something has actually happened within us through the work of the Spirit, and it is described as death *and* resurrection in Christ. The gift of salvation is what God does *in us* as well as what he does *for us*.

Look at the passage again. It goes on to point out what we already know to be true: there will be very real challenges as we try to live the new life. We are told that we must no longer let sin reign in our mortal bodies (vv. 12–13), but that we must offer ourselves to God to be "instruments of righteousness" (there's the theme of righteousness again). This is hard. How can we do such things? It will not happen by keeping rules in our own strength (the "law," v. 14), but because by grace we have become different people—we are "those who have been brought from death to life" (v. 13).

Later in chapters 6 and 7, Paul explains that being new people, dead to sin and alive in Christ, is the foundation for the new walk.

- In 6:16–18 he explains that we can live lives of "obedience [that] leads to righteousness" because we "*have been set free* from sin and *have become slaves* to righteousness."
- In 6:22 he says, "Now that you have been set free from sin and have become slaves to God, the benefit you reap leads to holiness [or *sanctification*], and the result is eternal life."
- In 7:4–6, Paul tells us that we died in order to belong "to him who was raised from the dead" so that "now, by dying to what once bound us, we have been released from the law so that we serve in the new way of the Spirit, and not in the old way of the written code."

BUT WHEN I WANT TO DO GOOD, SIN IS EVER PRESENT IN ME

This study can leave you very discouraged. The beauty of the resurrection life in Christ seems so far from our day-to-day struggle to be a faithful disciple. But if you read Paul's account of his own struggle in 7:14–25, you will find that Paul is very realistic about the battle that rages within the believer. Someone who has been born again has a new life in Christ, and yet the old life is still there, too. The question for Paul (and us) seems to be: "Will I focus on my own inadequacy or on the amazing truth that I have been brought into spiritual union with the risen Lord Jesus Christ?" In the end, that focus on Christ, made known in the gospel, will gradually transform us into Christ's image (2 Cor. 3:18).[1] I believe this is sanctification *by faith*. "Who will deliver me from this body of death?" That question has an answer for one who is alive in Christ: "Thanks be to God—through Jesus Christ our Lord!" (Rom. 7:25).

JUSTIFICATION (ROM. 3–5) AND SANCTIFICATION (ROM. 6–8): THEY GO TOGETHER, BUT THEY ARE DIFFERENT

A good way to grow in understanding of these two wonderful benefits of believing the gospel is to compare and contrast them. How are they alike and how are they different?

1. In 2 Corinthians 3:18 Paul uses "transformed" (Rom. 12:2) to describe what happens when a believer focuses heart and mind on Jesus. I explain this phenomenon in Day 38 of my book *Forty Days on the Mountain* (Wheaton, IL: Crossway Books, 2007).

- Both justification and sanctification are directly tied to the gospel story:
  - Justification ties us particularly to the crucifixion of Jesus.
  - Sanctification ties us particularly to the resurrection of Jesus.
- Both justification and sanctification are about the "righteousness of God" revealed in the gospel (1:17):
  - Justification is God's *declaring* us righteous.
  - Sanctification is God's *making* us righteous.
- Both justification and sanctification come by "God's free grace":[2]
  - Justification is an *act* of God's free grace (a declaration).
  - Sanctification is a *work* of God's free grace (a process).
- Both justification and sanctification are received by faith:
  - In justification we believe God's promise that his justice is satisfied because of the death of Christ.
  - In sanctification we believe God's promise that we are united to Christ in death for our sin and in resurrection for a new life.
- Both justification and sanctification have practical consequences:

2. Language of the Shorter Catechism (nos. 33–35).

- Because we are justified, we have peace with God and confidence to persevere in suffering.
- Because we are being sanctified, we have power to overcome our sin and live a new kind of life.

One truth should be very clear by now: salvation includes both justification and sanctification (and even more, as we will see). Don't confuse them, because our hope is based on Christ's righteousness imputed to us (justification), not how much progress

Time Out

Meet Dietrich Bonhoeffer.

Bonhoeffer was a German pastor and scholar who lived in the years leading up to World War II. He found that much of the church in his country had become totally satisfied with what they interpreted as Martin Luther's teaching about justification and took little interest in living out their faith. (They did not understand Luther properly.) In 1937 Bonhoeffer published a now-famous book called *The Cost of Discipleship*. In the book, Bonhoeffer introduced a phrase that has become well known: *cheap grace*. "Cheap grace is the deadly enemy of our church. We are fighting today for costly grace. . . . Cheap grace means grace as a doctrine, a principle, a system . . . the justification of sin without the justification of the sinner . . . the preaching of forgiveness without requiring repentance, baptism without church discipline, communion without confession. . . . Cheap grace is grace without we are making in living out our sanctification. But don't separate them, either. Jesus, revealed in the gospel, calls and forgives us, but he is the same Jesus whose power makes us different people.

SANCTIFICATION—LIFE IN THE SPIRIT

Romans 8 is one of the most remarkable chapters of this remarkable letter. No doubt you had the same sense when you

discipleship, grace without the cross, grace without Jesus Christ, living and incarnate."[1] *Couldn't cheap grace also be defined as trying to have justification without sanctification?*

Bonhoeffer remained a faithful disciple during the years of Adolf Hitler's domination in Germany. He was safe in the United States, but in 1939 he returned to Germany to lead his "Confessing Church," to resist Nazi teaching. He continued serving Christ until he was executed by Nazi prison guards shortly before the war ended. In *The Cost of Discipleship* Bonhoeffer wrote, "When Jesus calls a man, he bids him come and die."[2] These were not just words; Bonhoeffer, like many before and since, died because he was a faithful disciple of Jesus. This is a story that you should know about.[3]

1. Dietrich Bonhoeffer, *The Cost of Discipleship* (New York: Macmillan, 1963), 45–47.
2. Ibid., 99.
3. There is a helpful brief telling of Bonhoeffer's life and death in Charles Colson, *The Faith* (Grand Rapids: Baker Books, 2008), 117–23.

read it for your assignment. It is about the new life we have "in Christ." That life is also called "life in the Spirit" rather than living "according to the sinful nature" (Rom. 8:4).[3]

Read Your Bible: Romans 8:1–11

Just as I have said about the other passages you are reading, don't try to understand everything that is here right away. But notice that Paul is beginning to pull together the blessings of justification and sanctification, saying in 8:4 that "the righteous requirements of the law might be fully met in us [justification], who do not live [walk] according to the sinful nature [flesh] but according to the Spirit [sanctification]."

If you are like me, you don't often feel as though your life is being lived under the control of the Spirit. It seems that the sinful nature has far more power than it should. This is the struggle that every disciple faces. Even Paul had that battle, as he described in 7:14–25. But in the end he celebrated the fact that Jesus Christ our Lord is far more powerful than even our sin, and he could say, "Therefore, there is now no condemnation for those who are in Christ Jesus" (8:1). As long as we are in this mortal body, we will have this struggle, but there will come a time when the risen Christ will give new life not only to our spirits, as he does now, but also to our bodies (8:11).

ADOPTION INTO THE FAMILY OF GOD

Keep reading in Romans 8 because Paul takes us to the third, and perhaps most wonderful, of all the benefits of believ-

3. "Sinful nature" is how the NIV translates the word *flesh* to try to help us not to think only about our physical flesh and bones. It refers to our desire to live without God.

ing the gospel: *adoption*. We owe nothing to the old life; it only destroyed us. Instead, realize that the new life has brought us into a new family—we now belong to God as his adopted child with Jesus as our older brother. A great Bible teacher wrote that if justification is the *primary* blessing of the gospel, then adoption is the *highest* of the blessings.[4] Why would he say that? Think about it.

Read Your Bible: Romans 8:12–17

The human process of adoption has two basic parts. First, a legal transaction must take place. A judge will make a record to declare that a certain child is now the son or daughter of a certain couple. All of this is written in a book, and the child now has the family name and the rights that go with being a member of the family. But then comes the second part as the child is actually welcomed into the family, and day by day the love grows that gives the child a sense of belonging and security. Even though the legal reality is established, the relationship will take time.

In much the same way, think of adoption as bringing together justification (declared part of God's family, as a legal act) and sanctification (being made part of God's family, by the working of the Spirit). The word translated "adoption" or "sonship" in 8:15 carries both of those ideas. Paul literally says, "You have received the Spirit of *adoption unto sonship*." *Adoption* is the legal declaration; *sonship* is the new relationship that we have with God and his people. And notice that by the Spirit we now actually speak to God with the intimate term *Abba*. In the Hebrew language,

4. J. I. Packer, *Knowing God* (Downers Grove, IL: InterVarsity Press, 1973), 186ff.

the root of the word for *Father* is *Ab*. So a baby trying to learn to say that will babble, "Abba," much as an English-speaking child will say "Papa" or "Dada."

Time Out

Does this remind you of the Lord's Prayer?

It should. Every time we say, "Our Father, who art in heaven," we are reminded of our adoption in Christ. We speak to God with the same level of intimacy as Jesus did. Mark 14:36 records that the night before his crucifixion he spoke to God as *Abba*, but that was his usual way of speaking to his Father. And you and I have that same privilege! We speak to God as sons and daughters, not outsiders, and we are even "heirs of God and co-heirs with Christ" (Rom. 8:17). The next time you begin your prayer with "Our Father," stop and meditate on what that means for you.

ARE YOU LIVING LIKE AN ORPHAN?

"Are you living like a son or an orphan?" That was the penetrating question frequently asked by Jack Miller and other leaders of the renewal movement that he started, named *Sonship*. That name fit because Sonship's appeal was to men and women who were children of God through faith in Jesus Christ, but they were living like insecure orphans who needed to take care of themselves. They may have had a theological understanding of *adoption*, but they were not enjoying their *sonship*—the privileges of their new relationship with God.[5]

SUFFERING AND GLORY

We have just begun to think about the blessings that this amazing gift of adoption unto sonship brings. If you made a list of the blessings of adoption, would you include suffering? If you look back at Romans 8:17, you will see that it should be part of the list. As brothers and sisters of Christ, we are called to share in his sufferings in order that we may also share in his glory. This will be the topic of our next lesson on the benefits of believing the gospel.

Summary of Chapter 8

My summary will be the questions from the Shorter Catechism that describe the benefits that come in this life to those who are effectually called (nos. 32–36):

> *What benefits do they that are effectually called partake of in this life?*
>
> They that are effectually called do in this life partake of justification, adoption, and sanctification, and the several benefits which in this life do either accompany or flow from them.

5. Sonship is still a ministry of World Harvest Mission. The program that is designed for study in churches is called, appropriately, *Gospel Transformation*. Learn more at www.whm.org.

What is justification?

Justification is an act of God's free grace, wherein he pardons all our sins, and accepts us as righteous in his sight, only for the righteousness of Christ imputed to us, and received by faith alone.

What is adoption?

Adoption is an act of God's free grace, whereby we are received into the number, and have a right to all the privileges, of the sons of God.

What is sanctification?

Sanctification is the work of God's free grace, whereby we are renewed in the whole man after the image of God, and are enabled more and more to die unto sin, and live unto righteousness.

What are the benefits which in this life do accompany or flow from justification, adoption, and sanctification?

The benefits which in this life do accompany or flow from justification, adoption, and sanctification are: assurance of God's love, peace of conscience, joy in the Holy Spirit, growing and persevering in grace to the end of our lives.

Assignments

1. **Continue reading in your Bible.** To prepare for the next lesson, read Romans 8–11. Give particular attention to

the last half of chapter 8, verses 18–39. Then read Paul's letter to the Philippians. This letter will give you a good sense of Paul's attitude as he faced death because of his service for Christ.

2. **Continue learning to pray and write in your journal.**

3. **Follow up on earlier assignments.**

- Have you revised your spiritual autobiography? I hope you can add to it as you learn more about discipleship from this class and other experiences and reading.
- Have you made a profession of your faith and joined a Christ-centered church?
- Are you meeting with a small group in which you are encouraged and encourage others?

CHAPTER 9

A New Future: Glorification

ROMANS 8 has a very special place in memories of my earliest days as a disciple of Jesus. I'm not even sure that I thought of myself as a disciple at that point because I was very much a baby in the faith. After baptism and an initial commitment to Bible study and fellowship, I moved away from the church that had helped me to get started, and my walk with Christ almost disappeared. Thankfully, however, I never let go of my new habit of reading one chapter of the Bible every night before I went to sleep. That was a slender thread to hang my faith on, but I tried to keep reading even though I understood very little. I remember that one night my reading brought me to Romans 8, and I read the last two verses proclaiming that nothing in all creation "will be able to separate us from the love of God that is in Christ Jesus our Lord." As I read those verses, I knew that my new faith was something that God had begun and that there would somehow be a way back. How that happened is another story, but that night I went to sleep reassured that God's love was even greater than I had imagined.

This chapter will complete a study of the benefits that come to us when we believe the gospel. There are benefits not only in this life, but in a life to come, and so the second half of Romans 8 emphasizes two words: *hope* and *glory.*

SHARING IN CHRIST'S SUFFERING

We cannot have a serious consideration of discipleship and leave out the question of struggle and suffering. Think back to your reading of Mark. When Jesus was trying to prepare the new disciples for the fact of his coming death, he taught them that they, too, needed to prepare to die. He said, "If anyone would come after me, he must deny himself and take up his cross and follow me. For whoever wants to save his life will lose it, but whoever loses his life for me and for the gospel will save it" (Mark 8:34–35). Many thousands, perhaps millions, of men and women, such as Dietrich Bonhoeffer, have already lost their lives for the sake of Jesus and the gospel, and it is still happening today. But whether or not we die as martyrs, everyone who is a disciple of Jesus will share, on some level, the suffering of Jesus. Paul, as well as Jesus himself, makes this truth clear. In Romans 5 Paul taught that because we have been justified through faith, we can rejoice in the hope of the glory of God, including rejoicing in our sufferings (5:1–5). As we continue our reading of Romans 8, we learn more about what that means.

Read Your Bible: Romans 8:17–27

Do you ever feel that something is drastically wrong with the world in which we live? Whether that means personal tragedies, violence in our communities, or major natural disasters, we are confronted every day with the reality that this world is not the place it should be. Paul uses a powerful picture to describe this reality in verse 22—the pain of a woman in labor: "We know that the whole creation has been groaning as in the pains of childbirth right up to the present time." This is a reminder that this world has been under a curse since the time of the fall. And even though believers have begun to taste the blessings of God's salvation ("the firstfruits of the Spirit," v. 23), we also "groan inwardly."

Notice that Paul says we are groaning because we are waiting for our "adoption." But haven't we already learned about our adoption in 8:15–17? Don't those verses teach that it is *now* that "the Spirit himself testifies with our spirit that we are God's children" (v. 16)? What could it mean to say that we are waiting for our adoption? It means that the adoption we experience now is only a taste of our *full* adoption, which will include the "redemption of our bodies" (v. 23). What is amazing is that this final adoption is part of God's redeeming the whole creation: "The creation itself will be liberated from its bondage to decay and brought into the glorious freedom of the children of God" (v. 21).

How can all of this possibly happen? The answer comes to us through the gospel. As we know, the gospel is the story of Jesus, who came to bring peace, God's *shalom*, from heaven to earth. Jesus called this "the kingdom of God" (Mark 1:15). He accomplished it by going to war against Satan and the final enemy, death. He cast out demons, healed the sick, raised the dead, and faced death himself at the cross. And Jesus won! His death and resurrection marked the turning point in God's great plan to remove every aspect of the curse of sin. The war isn't over, but the outcome is certain, and the whole creation is waiting for the time when God completes what he plans to do for his children (Rom. 8:19) and Jesus returns to restore all things.

No wonder Paul can say that any suffering that we must endure while we wait cannot be compared to the glory that will follow (v. 18). This is the time when we wait, but with a hope as real as the resurrection of Jesus. And while we wait, we serve Jesus with the help of the Holy Spirit, who deepens our relationship to the Father (vv. 26–27).

CALLED ACCORDING TO HIS PURPOSE

There is another reason why we can live in the midst of a suffering world that will include our own suffering. Paul explains

Time Out

What about going to heaven when we die? Isn't that what salvation is all about?

The answer is yes and no. *Yes*, because the glorious future, which is our hope, is still future, and waits for the time of Christ's return to earth. There is still the question of what happens to followers of Jesus if they die before that time. The Bible teaches that at their death they will be in the presence of God. We think of the dwelling place of God as "heaven," and so "going to heaven" is a good way to describe what happens to a believer at death. Paul, expecting to die any day, wrote this to the Philippian church from prison: "I desire to depart and be with Christ." He also said, "For to me, to live is Christ and to die is gain" (Phil. 1:21–23).

But going to heaven is not "what salvation is all about." That is clear from Romans 8, and we could that all of this is part of the unfolding of God's will. The little part that any of us play is a piece of something greater than we can possibly imagine. In the next few verses Paul gives us a little peek into the mystery of God's eternal plan.

Read Your Bible: Romans 8:28–30

We started our study of discipleship with the call of Jesus. We saw the call again at the beginning of Romans. Now Paul adds to the idea by saying that we are "called *according to his purpose*." Our calling is the working out of God's plan ("those he predestined") because he has already known us ("those God

study many other passages that agree. God will one day make this earth a new place, and we are a part of the great renewal as we follow Jesus, even through times of suffering. I confess that I have struggled with the idea that my purpose in life is to wait around until I die so that I can go to heaven. Perhaps you have that same struggle. I think that idea is behind the message conveyed by so many sermons and gospel songs, but it is not the full picture. I wonder whether that is one reason why being a disciple is considered optional by many who call themselves Christian. Do people believe in Jesus just to get a ticket to heaven? There is more to the gospel and our hope for the future than going to heaven when we die. Jesus came to bring God's kingdom, and one day we will see and experience it in all its fullness and glory. That is our great hope.

foreknew") from all eternity. And if God has called us, he has also justified us; and if he has justified us, he has also glorified us (v. 30). WOW! What can we say to that? That is exactly the question Paul asks as the passage continues (v. 31).

Time Out

So what is glorification?

Glorification is the completion of the salvation that God began when he called us to himself. Romans 8:30 says that those he called and justified, "he also glorified." It is stated as though glorification were already ours. And it is! What God has planned will come to pass, and so we are already experiencing something of the glory that is ahead because we are "in Christ." The key to glorification is the resurrection of Jesus. The risen Christ gives new life to us now (regeneration and sanctification), but there is more. A time is coming when those who belong to Christ will also be raised up physically in the same kind of new body Jesus had at his resurrection. Jesus himself taught this truth (John 5:24–30), as did Paul (1 Cor. 15; 2 Cor. 4:7–5:10; Col. 3:1–4; 1 Thess. 4:13–18). The ultimate hope that Paul describes in Romans 8 waits for the return of Christ and the day of resurrection.

Whatever your background, whether you are a new or renewed disciple, you can appreciate that this mystery of God's predestination is a truly awesome thing. Don't try to "figure this out," because it won't happen—this is God's revealing his *sovereignty* (which is a word meaning "nothing higher," "answering to no one").[1] Paul's intention here is to bring together all the pieces of our salvation (such as calling, justification, and glorification) to give us a look at the bigger picture—not to confuse us but to give us even greater hope—that God, who has an eternal purpose for all his creation, is *for us*! What more could we ask for?

WHAT CAN WE SAY TO ALL THIS?

Don't miss the fact that God's purpose is very clear. It is that we become "conformed to the likeness of his Son" (Rom. 8:29). The "good" that God is doing in our lives is making us more like Jesus. Romans 8:28 is often quoted to assure people that all things work together for *our* good, meaning that God's will is always that we be happy, healthy, and prosperous. That is *not* the meaning of the text. Do those things serve the purpose of making us more like Christ? If so, then God could indeed use them for good. But if suffering or persecution or famine or sword serves God's purpose, then he will send those. Read carefully the last verses of Romans 8, and pay particular attention to how many questions Paul asks to close out this amazing chapter.

Read Your Bible: Romans 8:31–39

Have you ever attended a live performance of the *1812 Overture* by Pyotr Ilyich Tchaikovsky? He wrote it to celebrate

1. I offer a brief explanation of the doctrine in my booklet *What Is a Reformed Church?* (Phillipsburg, NJ: P&R Publishing, 2003), 11–17.

the victory of the Russian army over Napoleon on the outskirts of Moscow. The music is full of life and celebration, but when it comes time for the climax, everything breaks loose. The bells ring, the drums and cymbals crash, and over all the instruments the cannons start to roar. It is a thrilling piece of music. When I read these verses in Romans 8, I think of the *1812 Overture*. One question leads to an answer that jumps to another question and then an answer. The joy seems to tumble out as Paul writes:

- If God is for us, who can be against us?
- If God gave his Son for us, will he not freely give us all things?
- Why should we have any fear on the day of judgment when God the Father has chosen us and Christ is there to defend us?
- And what could possibly stop us in this life? Yes it will be hard, but . . .
- We are more than conquerors through him who loved us.
- Therefore, nothing—nothing in our past, present, or future, whether we can see it or not, nothing in all creation—will be able to separate us from the love of God that is ours in Christ Jesus.

ASSURANCE OF SALVATION

The last two verses of Romans 8, which meant so much to me as a young, struggling believer, draw us to Paul's conclusion of what it means that God has graciously given us salvation in Jesus Christ. We are saved in the present, but it is an eternal salvation: "The wages of sin is death, but the gift of God is eternal life in Christ Jesus our Lord" (Rom. 6:23). The benefit of those verses to me that night, I now realize, is called *assurance of salvation*. It was the whisper of the Holy Spirit testifying to my spirit that I was God's child (8:16). It is possible not only to have peace with God, but to *know* we are at peace with God. This is not presumption (although it certainly can be without a heartfelt desire to follow Jesus); it is faith. We believe and rest on God's promises that come to us in the gospel.

One of the traditional confessions that is said together in many churches at the beginning of communion is: "Christ has died, Christ is risen, Christ is coming again, Hallelujah!" The people then receive the bread and wine to bear witness that their trust for salvation is in Christ whom they confessed. Every observance of communion is an opportunity to reaffirm our hope in Christ alone.[2]

For Reflection

Have you come to the place in your journey with Christ that you feel assured that his salvation is yours? Write down your thoughts or talk about this in your group. Assurance of salvation is a privilege that is yours as a disciple of Jesus. It will free you to follow him joyfully into whatever struggles are ahead

2. The apostle John not only wrote a gospel, but also wrote a short letter called 1 John (toward the end of the New Testament) to help new believers be assured that they were born of God. Read it when you get a chance.

because you know that nothing can separate you from the love of God that is in Christ Jesus your Lord.

PUTTING THE PIECES TOGETHER

I know that I have probably filled your plate with much more than you can take in right now. Keep in mind, however, that Romans was written to a *young* church full of new and renewed disciples just like you. Paul understood that they could read his writings and discuss them together again and again, and that is my expectation as well. There will always be more to learn. I have taught these passages many times, but preparing these studies has opened my eyes to new depths of the gospel. One of the most fundamental aspects of growing as disciples of Jesus is a never-ending desire to learn about him and what he is calling us to do. So I emphasize again, take your time and let the gospel soak into your soul.

Here is a diagram that I hope will help to put the pieces of the gospel together for you.[3] Keep in mind that the core truth of everything we are studying is our spiritual union with Christ in his death and resurrection (represented by the X in the center of the wheel). None of these great benefits of salvation—calling, conversion, justification, sanctification, adoption, glorification—have any meaning apart from the fact that they are ours "in Christ," who is revealed in the gospel. This means that we are back to the gospel as the foundation of our life in Christ.

3. The idea for this wheel diagram came from reading John Murray, *Redemption, Accomplished and Applied* (Grand Rapids: Eerdmans, 1955). The final diagram is my adaptation.

Fig. 6. Salvation by Grace

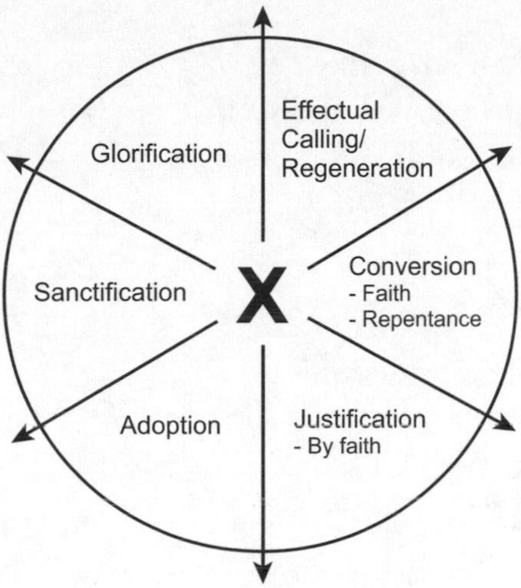

Summary of Chapter 9

Discipleship cannot be discussed without also considering the matter of suffering; but Romans 8 teaches that suffering will be nothing compared to the glory that will follow:

- The whole creation struggles under the curse.
- When Christ returns to raise his people from the dead, all of creation will also be redeemed.
- Going to heaven when we die is only part of the picture.

Called according to his purpose:

- We are known by God and predestined.
- Those he predestined are called, justified, and glorified.

- Glorification is the completion of our salvation—it is tied to what happened to Jesus at the resurrection.

What can we say to this? WOW!
- God's purpose is clear—to make us become like Christ, our older brother.
- Paul poses a series of dramatic questions.
- Nothing can separate us from the love of God in Christ.

Assurance of salvation:
- We rest in Christ alone.

Putting the pieces together:
- The wheel.

Assignments

1. **Continue to read your Bible regularly.** To prepare for the next lesson, read Romans 12–14. Begin reading Acts of the Apostles. This book tells the story of Jesus' beginning to build his church in the decades after his resurrection and ascension. Make a plan to finish reading Acts by the time you study chapter 12 of this book.

2. **Write in your journal.** What are your thoughts about your sense of the assurance of salvation? Are you writing down the questions that come as you read your Bible and prepare the lessons?

STEPS IN THE WALK OF DISCIPLESHIP

Step One: Know the gospel itself

Step Two: Know how you came to believe the gospel

Step Three: Know the benefits of believing the gospel (gospel doctrines)

✗ **Step Four: Live a life that flows from the gospel (gospel obedience)**

CHAPTER 10

Faith Expressing Itself in Love

IN THE FIRST LESSON of *The Walk* we met Levi, who was sitting at the tax collector's booth minding his own business (which was everyone else's business, too). Jesus walked up to the man, whom he was seeing for the first time as far as we know, and spoke a single command: "Follow me." And we are told that Levi got up and followed him.

In his book *The Cost of Discipleship*, Dietrich Bonhoeffer (remember him?) has this to say about Jesus' call of Levi: "The call goes forth, and it is at once followed by the response of obedience. The response of the disciples is an act of obedience, not a confession of faith in Jesus. How could the call immediately evoke obedience?"[1] Bonhoeffer explains that the reason any of us respond to the call "is Jesus Christ himself. . . . Jesus summons men to follow him, not as a teacher or a pattern of the good life, but as the Christ, the Son of God."[2] And when

1. Dietrich Bonhoeffer, *The Cost of Discipleship* (New York: Macmillan, 1963), 61.
2. Ibid., 62.

Jesus calls, we come—and we follow him. If we understand this, there is no conflict between faith and obedience. In his first words to the Roman church, Paul talked about his mission "to call people from among all the Gentiles to *the obedience that comes from faith*" (Rom. 1:5). Paul ends Romans with exactly the same phrase, although in the NIV it is translated "that all nations might *believe and obey* him" (16:26).

This brings us to step four of discipleship through the gospel: gospel obedience. I call it *gospel* obedience because there can certainly be an approach to obedience that is defined simply as "doing our duty," or "keeping the rules." Doing the right thing for the wrong reasons does not honor Christ. Nor does obedience as an effort to repay God for his salvation, as though we could make ourselves worthy of his great love and grace. But there is a natural fruit that grows from a Spirit-given faith in the gospel, and it is what Paul calls the "obedience that comes from faith." This is when the gospel becomes visible in lives and we begin to learn what it means to say, "The gospel changes everything."

In your reading of Romans 12, did you notice how naturally Paul moves from his extended teaching about God's mercy to the challenge of obedience?[3] We are urged to offer ourselves as living sacrifices. We are called to this act of obedience not to earn God's mercy, but because of it.

Read Your Bible: Romans 11:33–12:8

3. I intentionally did not try to look at Romans 9–11. It is an important, involved discussion of God's plan to set aside his people the Jews because they were seeking to establish their own righteousness. He did this to open the way for those who receive righteousness through faith, whether Jew or Gentile, by believing the gospel (10:1–15 is a good summary passage).

LIFE IN THE COMMUNITY OF BELIEVERS

You should have noticed in your reading that Paul wrote assuming that his readers were part of a "body," which is one of the common ways in which the New Testament describes a church. This reinforces the point I first made in chapter 2 that there is no thought on the part of Jesus or Paul or other writers of Scripture that we can be disciples on our own. We carry out our calling as members of a fellowship of believers.

Romans 12 begins with the charge to every brother (and sister) to offer to God our bodies as living sacrifices. This dedication of our total beings is pleasing to God and received by him as an act of worship. I have heard this text preached on many times, and the standard joke is that the problem with *living* sacrifices is that they constantly want to climb off the altar. How true!

Dedicating ourselves to God in this way means that:

- We stop conforming to the pattern of this world (habits, actions, and attitudes that reflect the old life without Christ). One translation of this thought is "don't let the world around you squeeze you into its own mold."[4]
- We begin to be transformed (this is the word *metamorphosis* that we use to describe the transformation of the caterpillar into a butterfly) by the renewing of our minds. This will come about as we learn to fix our

4. *The New Testament in Modern English*, trans. J. B. Phillips (New York: Macmillan, 1958).

minds on Christ and let our thinking be shaped by the Word of God.
- We view ourselves with humility, not arrogance, when we serve in Jesus' church.

Paul then introduces the important truth that if the church is the body of Christ, we are one, and yet every member, just like parts of the human body, has a different part to play in the overall health of the body. These are called "gifts," and there are several lists of these gifts in different letters to churches. (1 Corinthians 12 is another example.) Notice that Paul lists seven basic gifts in this passage:

- Prophesying (preaching or proclaiming the Word of God).
- Service.
- Teaching.
- Encouraging others.
- Contribution of money.
- Leadership (administration).
- Showing mercy.

Does any one of these gifts seem to suit what you have to give to your church? This list is not intended to set out the only gifts we can bring, but it does challenge us to prayerfully consider what we can do for the overall health of the church. Often you will discover your gift(s) only as you become involved in the ministry of your congregation. Write down some thoughts about this, or talk about it in your group.

THE ONLY THING THAT COUNTS IS LOVE

All the different obligations expected of a disciple can be summed up in a single word. It is *love*. The famous chapter on love, 1 Corinthians 13, appears in the midst of a discussion of the use and misuse of gifts in the church. Our prophecy or gifts to the poor, or even faith, are meaningless apart from love (1 Cor. 13:2). Almost every list of godly virtues in the New Testament begins or ends with love. After arguing with the Galatians about their desertion of the gospel for a religion of works, Paul made this remarkable statement: "The only thing that counts is faith expressing itself through love" (Gal. 5:6). As you continue reading in Romans 12, notice that the passage begins with love.

Read Your Bible: Romans 12:9–21

As you read through the passage, can you begin to understand why a small group of people who took these commands seriously could change the world? At first the disciples of Jesus were despised as weak, but slowly their acts of kindness toward one another and their neighbors stood out in total contrast to the greed and hatred of the world. People were drawn, like our friend Titus, to learn more about the Jesus whom these Christians were following. The spread of the church is a remarkable story, and behind that story is the story of *faith expressing itself through love*.

You read in Romans 12:9, "Love [*agape*] must be sincere." You could put that sentence in bold, followed by statements that provide specific examples of what love looks like. Notice in verse 10 that "brotherly love" (*philos*) is part of how we love. Love even allows us to not take revenge but live at peace with everyone (if it is possible), and to be kind to our enemies (12:17–19). How can we do this? This kind of love is something that only Jesus could express. Exactly the point! Our love to others is an overflow of the love we have experienced in Jesus. And he has called us to follow him. This

Time Out

What do you mean when you talk about love?

Great question. It is very important that we have a proper understanding of what love is. The New Testament is very clear about what it means. The Greek language had three primary words for *love. Eros* spoke of passionate love. Often this knew no bounds, and our word *erotic* comes from that root. But it always spoke of love driven by feelings. To be "in love" is *eros. Philos*, on the other hand, was a word used for friendship or affection—what we often speak of as "liking" someone. I live in *Phil*adelphia—the city of "brotherly love." The third word for *love* is *agape.* When I demonstrate *agape* love, I want what is best for a person, and I will work and even sacrifice to fulfill my love. The older versions of the English Bible often translated the word as "charity," to demonstrate that *agape* meant doing something good for others.

It would probably not surprise you to learn that while the word seldom appears in the secular Greek writing of the day, *agape* is the most commonly used word for *love* in the New Testament. When "God so *loved* the world" (John 3:16), he did something to show that love: he sent his Son.

means that he can command us to love our enemies. It doesn't mean that we necessarily like them, but we will work for their good (12:21). This is *agape*—love that is an act of obedience.

LOVE—THE FULFILLMENT OF THE LAW

Now that you understand the nature of biblical love, you can also understand that love is not in opposition to the truth of God and his law. When love is just "sentimentality," as Lewis calls it, and we "love" by following our feelings or what the other person is asking for, that course can actually be destructive. Many well-meaning parents have learned that lesson the hard way. Love calls for us to do what is right and best for the person we love; this is what is often called "tough love" today. Thankfully, we have real guidance about what tough love means—it is explained in God's law. Read another section of Romans where Paul makes this point.

Read Your Bible: Romans 13:8–10

Remember that how the word *law* is used must be understood in its setting (or its "context"). *Law* can refer just to the Old Testament (Rom. 3:21) or a legalistic view of keeping all the Old Testament laws ("you are not under law but under grace," 6:14). But in this passage, the word refers to what is called the "moral law" as summarized in the Ten Commandments. Clearly, Paul does not think the moral law is to be disregarded. These laws are fulfilled by love, and the reverse is true as well: I learn how to love by keeping the law. For example, if I love my neighbor, I won't steal from him, commit adultery with his wife, and so on. The church through the centuries has received the Ten Commandments as

Time Out

Meet C. S. Lewis.

C. S. Lewis was a British scholar of classic literature who lived in the last century. He stumbled into faith through reading great literature and discovering that the best thinking and imagination belonged to Christians. Once he was converted, Lewis used his gift of writing to affect multitudes of readers, and he is still widely read. The books in his fantasy series *The Chronicles of Narnia* are currently appearing as very popular movie adaptations (*The Lion, the Witch and the Wardrobe* and *Prince Caspian*). As a new or renewed disciple, you would benefit from reading Lewis's *Screwtape Letters*, in which an under-devil writes to his nephew, "Wormwood," who is a lesser devil, about how to undermine the faith of a new believer.

Lewis is perhaps best known for his book *Mere Christianity*, which was originally a series of BBC

God's expanding on what it means to keep the two great commandments: love to God and love for neighbor.[5]

The preface:

> "I am the LORD your God, who brought you out of Egypt, out of the land of slavery."

5. Jesus said this in Mark 12:30–31, but keep in mind that he was quoting from the Old Testament (Deut. 6:5; Lev. 19:18). Don't make the common mistake of thinking about the Old Testament only as law and the New Testament only as love.

radio talks in the 1940s. In the chapter on charity, he had this to say about the matter of acting with love whether or not we like the person: "Do not waste time bothering whether you 'love' your neighbor; act as if you did. . . . Consequently, though Christian charity sounds a very cold thing to people whose heads are full of sentimentality, and though it is quite distinct from affection, yet it leads to affection. The difference between a Christian and a worldly man is not that the worldly man has only affections or 'likings' and the Christian has only 'charity'. The worldly man treats certain people kindly because he 'likes' them; the Christian, trying to treat everyone kindly, finds himself liking more and more people as he goes on—including people he could not even have imagined himself liking at the beginning."[1]

1. C. S. Lewis, *Mere Christianity* (New York: Collier Books, 1960), 116–17.

How to love God (first four commandments):

1. "You shall have no other gods before me."
2. "You shall not make for yourself an idol . . ."
3. "You shall not misuse the name of the Lord your God . . ."
4. "Remember the Sabbath day by keeping it holy."

How to love our neighbor (six commandments):

5. "Honor your father and your mother . . ."
6. "You shall not murder."

7. "You shall not commit adultery."
8. "You shall not steal."
9. "You shall not give false testimony . . ."
10. "You shall not covet . . ."

(Ex. 20:1–17; Deut. 5:1–22)

Time Out

You need to learn the Ten Commandments.

The Ten Commandments were given to God's people after the exodus, when they were delivered from slavery in Egypt. They are not really "rules," but ten eternal principles by which God revealed how to live in a way that would not send the Israelites back into another form of bondage. The Ten Commandments are basic because God was speaking to those who were children in terms of their experience of God. Pay close attention to the preface—it is very important because it reminds us of who God is. Just as we begin our praying by remembering that we are speaking to "our Father, who art in heaven," the preface reminds us that the God who gives the commandments is the same God who delivered his people from slavery. The commandments appear above in brief form.

GET READY FOR A BATTLE—CLOTHE YOURSELVES WITH JESUS

As we take seriously the call to follow Jesus in gospel obedience, we must prepare for the fact that we are following Jesus into enemy territory. There is not much that the enemies of

Jesus can do to him, as he proved, but they will go after his followers if they can. Traditionally, the Christian church has identified the enemies of Jesus' disciples as *the world*, *the flesh*, and *the devil*. Consider them briefly.

The world. This does not mean the earth, or the world of people, but a world system. It is an approach to life that leaves out God. "The world" may be very sensual, but it can also be materialism, secularism, or any number of other *-isms* that are the idols of our modern world. Remember that part of being a living sacrifice is that we stop conforming to the pattern of the world (Rom. 12:2).

The flesh. As we have already noted, *the flesh* does not refer to our bodies, but that part of us that is a remnant of our core sinful nature.[6] We will not be rid of the flesh until God takes it away at death or the day of resurrection. The flesh is like an antenna that connects us with the world and makes it still attractive even after we have encountered Jesus.

The devil. The Bible is very clear that there is an ancient enemy of all that has to do with God. He is the devil, or Satan. Hell is a place created for Satan (Matt. 25:41). The realm of evil and the demonic is very mysterious, and we are warned just to stay away. In some cultures the satanic presence seems to be more overt, but in other cultures that presence is much more subtle. No doubt Satan prefers to stay hidden because those who make little of him will also make little of Christ. The first disciples learned, however, that Jesus could cast out demons with a word (they heard demons begging Jesus for mercy, Mark 5:12). The

6. Reminder: This is how the NIV translates "flesh."

disciples learned that they were safe when they were with Jesus, and that is our lesson as well.

CLOTHE YOURSELVES WITH THE LORD JESUS CHRIST

Read Your Bible: Romans 13:11–14

We must be realistic about the struggle with the world, the flesh, and the devil. These three enemies are each strong enough to destroy us, and together they are impossible to defeat in our own strength. But we *can* remain faithful and effective disciples by keeping Jesus central in our lives and minds. Think of his righteousness, revealed through the gospel, as that "armor of light" we put on (Rom. 13:12). That may sound simplistic, but it is a fundamental principle of living for Christ. Over and over, disciples of Jesus stumble and fall because they try to discipline themselves to change and "do better next time." The more you focus on your sin—even in your desire to be free from it—the more power it will have over you. "Rather, clothe yourselves with the Lord Jesus Christ" (13:14), and you will begin to experience that "renewing of your mind" that frees you from conforming "to the pattern of this world" (12:2).

Do you remember the first step in discipleship through the gospel? It is to stay focused on the gospel itself (chapter 4). The gospel reveals Jesus in all his majestic glory, and by faith we have put on the Lord Jesus Christ. Look again at Romans 13:14 because that is the only way we begin to overcome all the junk of the old life—if we "clothe [ourselves] with the

Lord Jesus Christ," we will find that our minds are not so drawn to things of the flesh.

For Reflection

Stop and think about this fundamental principle for your own life with Jesus. Do you understand that there is a difference between trying harder to overcome your sins and struggles by your own effort, and learning to focus on Jesus revealed in the gospel so that in Christ you find power to overcome? It is a very important difference. Talk about this with others.

Summary of Chapter 10

Step four of discipleship through the gospel—gospel obedience—is obedience that comes from faith. The call to dedicate our lives to obedient service flows naturally from Paul's long discussion of the gospel mercy.

Life in community:

- Participation in the church is assumed as Paul begins to define the obedience of faith.
- Consider what gift you might have to strengthen the body of Christ.

Love must be sincere:

- Love is the summary of all we are commanded to do.
- *Love* is *agape* love—a word of action and commitment.

Love is the fulfillment of the law:

- Learn the Ten Commandments.

Clothe yourselves with Jesus Christ to overcome the enemies of our faith:

- The world, the flesh, and the devil are powerful, but not stronger than Jesus.

Assignments

1. **Continue to read your Bible regularly.** Complete the reading of Romans to prepare for the next lesson. Continue reading Acts. This should help you get a bigger picture of the world in which the church was birthed.

2. **Memorize the Ten Commandments.** Just like the Lord's Prayer, the Ten Commandments need to be burned into your consciousness. They are a remarkable resource for wisdom in making difficult decisions.

3. **Think more deeply about the matter of spiritual gifts.** You should talk about this with people in your congregation who have gotten to know you. Often others will give us good insight into how we can serve the body of Christ. Do some writing about this.

CHAPTER 11

The Gospel Changes Everything

YOU ARE NOW A MISSIONARY

I'm sure that when Jesus called those first disciples to follow him, they had no idea of what that call meant. The call was to follow Jesus, and that is what they did. They followed him as he healed diseases, cast out demons, fed the hungry, and taught in a way that astounded the people and angered the religious authorities. Finally Jesus went to the cross as a result of human hatred for him, but also because doing so was the will of God. And then God blew away the forces of death and hell by raising Christ from the dead and receiving him back into heaven.

What do you think was going on in the minds and hearts of those first disciples as the gospel story unfolded in the life and ministry of Jesus? You have been learning more and more about Jesus and what it means to walk step by step on the path of discipleship. Now we need to consider another important meaning of discipleship—the mission. Jesus came on a mission and called his disciples to join him on that mission. Remember that this is what Jesus said when he called Peter and Andrew, James and John? He said, "Come, follow me, . . . and I will make you fishers of men" (Mark 1:17). He was talking to men who fished for a living, and he was telling them that the direction and purpose of their lives would now be different.

Are you a disciple of Jesus? Have you responded to his call to follow him? Then you, too, have a new purpose for your life. You are on a mission—*which makes you a missionary!* Seriously! Think about it—a missionary is someone on a mission, and every disciple of Jesus is called to be part of his mission. So the question becomes, what does it mean for *you* to be a missionary?

There are at least two important ways in which every disciple can be part of Jesus' mission:

- *By learning to bring all things under the lordship of Jesus.* We must learn to see the world and life from God's perspective and shape our lives around that perspective. That is the central point of this chapter.
- *By participating in Jesus' mandate to "make disciples of the nations."* We get involved in the worldwide spread of the gospel by making disciples wherever we are. This will be the focus of the final chapter.

TRANSFORMED BY THE RENEWING OF OUR MINDS

Read once more the key verses for gospel obedience, Romans 12:1–2:

> Therefore I urge you, brothers, in view of God's mercy, to offer your bodies as living sacrifices, holy and pleasing to God—this

> is your spiritual act of worship. Do not conform any longer to the pattern of this world, but be transformed by the renewing of your mind. Then you will be able to test and approve what God's will is—his good, pleasing, and perfect will.

Did you notice that a key part of dedicating ourselves as living sacrifices is *the renewing of our minds*? This means that because of God's mercy to us through Christ, not only are our hearts changed, but we begin to *think* differently. First of all, we have a new understanding about Jesus—he is now our Lord and Savior and King. Our focus on Jesus is the primary way in which we are *being transformed* by the renewing of our minds. Remember that the word for *transformed* is the same as *metamorphosis*. This is the same word that is used in 2 Corinthians 3:18, to tell how we are transformed into the likeness of Christ by beholding his glory through the gospel.

Having our minds renewed also means that we begin to look at all of life differently. Keep in mind that as unbelievers we have been looking at God's world from a very selfish point of view. *What would that world look like if we could see it through God's eyes?* That is one of the great values in regularly reading the Bible. Not everything you read will apply directly to you, but you will gradually gain a view of life that reflects God's perspective. This is called a *biblical worldview*, or a *Christian worldview*. All people have a way in which they view the world, even if they can't explain it.[1] As disciples of Jesus, we must pray for the renewing of our minds to bring our thinking into conformity with God's will rather than the world, and then live a life that fulfills that worldview. "The reason the church fails to have a transforming influence on our

1. Philip Graham Ryken, *What Is the Christian Worldview?* (Phillipsburg, NJ: P&R Publishing, 2006), 6.

Time Out

Meet Charles Colson.

Charles Colson was a very determined and ruthless politician who was part of the government of the United States under President Richard Nixon in the 1970s. God broke into his life, and "Chuck" had a very dramatic conversion to Christ.[1] His old life caught up to him, however, and when arrested and indicted, he pleaded guilty to misuse of government power, and went to jail for several months. I remember reading a newspaper interview with Chuck shortly after news that he had been "born again" became public. At the end of the interview, he was asked what was different now that he had come to trust Christ. He answered that

1. Chapter 6 of my book *Spiritual Birthline: Understanding How We Experience the New Birth* (Wheaton, IL: Crossway Books, 2006) analyzes Chuck's conversion experience.

culture is that we do not know and do not live out the Bible-based, Christ-centered, Spirit-empowered, God-glorifying worldview that belongs to us by grace."[2] Our study of Romans introduces us to several examples of this new worldview.

SUBMIT TO THE GOVERNING AUTHORITIES

An important example of the biblical worldview is the discussion of earthly government in Romans 13. God's work in the world goes beyond what he does through the church. Even a government

2. Ibid., 11.

he now understood that Washington was not the real center of power, as he had once thought. Reading that statement told me that this was a different man—he wasn't just "religious," but his whole view of the world had been radically changed.

When Chuck left prison, he immediately started Prison Fellowship, a ministry that is now the largest prison ministry in the world. Prison Fellowship is a great example of how the gospel begins with personal change, and then flows into families and communities. As he grew in his faith, Chuck also became passionate to help Christians *think* as Christians, and he has done a great deal of writing about the biblical worldview. If you want a helpful source for a Christian perspective on all of life, become acquainted with the work of Charles Colson.[2]

2. A good place to start would be www.breakpoint.org.

that is unfriendly to the gospel has still been established by God to maintain justice. Try to read this passage through the eyes of believers in Rome. They were threatened by the earthly authority, and yet that authority was there by the will of God. Notice that three times government officials are called "God's servants."

Read Your Bible: Romans 13:1–7

This passage could lead to a discussion of human authority, the police powers of the state, paying taxes, and so on. You will want to think about those matters later. For now, however, use the passage as one example of how followers of Jesus look at the world differently. It helps us understand that God rules over all the world—whether or not people acknowledge his rule. In the end, God's purpose is fulfilled in all of life.

LET NO DEBT REMAIN OUTSTANDING

Another example of how followers of Jesus view life differently is the matter of money and possessions. In a very brief reference, Paul says that the only debt that we should have is the debt to love one another (Rom. 13:8). This is a reminder that how we handle our money is part of our discipleship. In fact, from a biblical perspective it is not *our* money—it is God's. We are to be stewards, or managers, of what God has given to us. This is the important theme of *stewardship*. Part of good stewardship is generosity in giving (12:8), but we are also called to be good managers of *all* that God has given us. As the text suggests, it is poor stewardship if we are in bondage to debt and unable to follow Jesus in new directions. In an important statement about money, Jesus told his disciples, "If you have not been trustworthy in handling worldly wealth, who will trust you with true riches?" (Luke 16:11). In other words, our stewardship of earthly possessions is a good test of how we will handle the greater gifts of God. Jesus went on to say, "No servant can serve two masters. Either he will hate the one and love the other, or he will be devoted to the one and despise the other. You cannot serve both God and Money" (16:13).

How does this speak to your attitude ("mind") about money and possessions? Do you recognize God as the real owner of all you have? What steps could you take to begin to be a faithful disciple of Jesus in the matter of material things? Think about it and talk about it.

VOCATION

Some application forms have a space for you to fill in your "vocation." What is expected is that you state what your job is. Are you a teacher or a lawyer or a student? But originally the word *vocation* meant "calling."

Time Out

Does this mean that I can't be a fisherman (or teacher or doctor or farmer) anymore?

Not at all. Some people, it is true, are called to leave their fishing to become preachers or teachers. But Jesus wants most of his disciples to stay home and be fishermen or carpenters or mothers (or even tax collectors!) *for the glory of God.* A disciple of Jesus should look at his or her "job" as a calling and therefore seek to do it in a way that reflects the character of Jesus. For example, someone called to be a police officer is actually identified as God's servant (Rom. 13:4). How wonderful to have such a servant who will not abuse his power, will not take bribes, and will truly care for the weak and helpless members of society! Our world needs those who fulfill their calling as disciples of Jesus by serving in the police force. Apply that same idea to artists and bankers and nurses and bus drivers and students.

This is another way to understand the calling of God. The effectual call, as we have seen, brings us to salvation and discipleship. But God also calls us to live out that call in different ways. Paul, for example, was "called to be an apostle" (Rom. 1:1), but not everyone has that calling. As a disciple of Jesus, you, too, need to see your life as a calling from God. For most of us, that will not be anything as dramatic as the call to be an apostle, but our calling will be to live out our discipleship in fairly ordinary ways.

Look at the last chapter of Romans, and the list of people Paul greeted. These were people he knew who were now part of the church in Rome. At the end of the list are also the names of people who sent greetings to the church of Rome. Don't try to study all the details, but just get a sense of the community of disciples, each serving one another in the body and then going out to serve Jesus in the world, such as Erastus, who was the city's director of public works (16:23). Notice that many of the disciples mentioned are women. While it seems clear that the offices of pastor and elder were to be fulfilled by godly *men* (1 Tim. 3), it is also clear that Paul was eager to include women in the work of the church.

Read Your Bible: Romans 16:1–23

We can understand calling in three ways:

- We are *all* called to follow Jesus, which we do by repenting and having faith in Jesus alone and living a life of obedience that comes from faith.
- We are *all* called to serve Jesus and one another in the body of Christ. We have "gifts" that contribute to the health and strength of our particular fellowship.

Time Out

Meet Jonah Kule.

Jonah is a wonderful example of a person who understood his work as a calling from God. He grew up in the very poor community of Bundibugyo in the western part of Uganda, Africa. He became a follower of Jesus as a young man and began to serve Jesus by dispensing medicine in a local clinic. He then became an assistant to two missionary doctors who were living in his town. Jonah's integrity encouraged these doctors to find the resources to send Jonah to medical school—the first person from his district in over thirty years to do so. He went to school in his mid-thirties and excelled over many younger students. When he graduated, he turned down several attractive offers in order to return and serve his own people. The people of Bundibugyo came to love "their doctor," although Jonah was not liked by some of the other doctors because he would not accept extra fees for his service. He believed that God had called him to serve, and that God would provide for his needs.

When reports came of a mysterious disease that was sickening many in a remote village, Jonah was the first to go. Instead of the cholera he expected, it turned out to be an outbreak of the dreadful Ebola virus. Thankfully, the virus was contained within a few weeks, but it took the life of Dr. Jonah Kule on December 4, 2007. He knew he was dying, but his last words reflected his thoughts of others: "I am going to die now," he said, "and I pray that no one should ever have to die of this disease again."[1]

1. Reported in the blog of Drs. Scott and Jennifer Myrhe: http://paradoxuganda.blogspot.com.

- We *all* have a vocation, a calling, to serve Jesus in this world. We should not separate what God is calling us to do in daily life from our discipleship. All that we have and all that we do is to be dedicated to our service to Christ.

What is your vocation at this point in your life? Have you been thinking about what you do in daily life as part of being a disciple? Are there some steps you can take to bring more of a biblical worldview into the work you are doing? Think about it and talk about it.

THE WEAK AND THE STRONG

A renewed mind will give a disciple of Jesus a special concern for the weak and needy. In the "flesh" we want to know how to be stronger than those around us. We want to win at whatever the cost, and the worst thing is to be thought of as a "loser." But in order to become disciples of Jesus, we must humble ourselves in repentance, and out of that "weakness" we discover true strength in Christ. And now because Christ is the Lord, we don't need to lord it over others.

In chapter 14 Paul applies this idea to the problem of weaker believers who were offended by other believers because of their eating practices (these could be Jewish believers who stopped eating only "kosher"), and because of how they observed special days (these could be Gentiles who weren't keeping a Jewish Sabbath). In some things there is no clear right and wrong—but it *is* wrong to ignore the concerns of the weak. Love for others must prevail over things such as eating and drinking: "Do not destroy the work of God for the sake of food. . . . We who are strong ought to bear with the failings of the weak and not to please ourselves. . . . Accept one another, then, just as Christ accepted you" (Rom. 14:20; 15:1, 7).

Read Your Bible: Romans 14:15–15:4

Think about how this principle of the strong serving the weak affects our worldview and actions:

- There is a particular concern for children—whether born or unborn. Early Christians rescued babies who were left exposed to die (an ancient substitute for abortion).
- The poor are cared for. Christians made sure that there were no needy persons within their own fellowship, and they also tried to be helpful to other neighbors. Sometimes just giving money is not the most helpful thing, so the Christian church has given thought to and expended energy in helping the poor learn to support themselves.
- The sick, disabled, and dying have always had a special place of ministry in the church. Many churches have a strong commitment to ministries of mercy that look for ways to serve the needy.
- There are peacemaking and racial reconciliation. When a Christian worldview has become part of the church (and sadly there are many examples of Christians' reflecting the racism and hatreds of this world), followers of Jesus have been leaders in bringing down barriers that separate people from one another.

IT'S THE GOSPEL

Are you beginning to understand the phrase "the gospel changes everything"? I first began hearing that phrase in association with the ministry of Redeemer Presbyterian Church in New York City. Led by its pastor, Dr. Tim Keller, Redeemer is having a remarkable impact on a very secular city, and the lessons being learned have been applied to churches in other great cities all over the world. This is Redeemer's vision: "Seeking to renew the city socially, spiritually and culturally."[3] How is Redeemer doing it? Its members are determined to stay centered in Christ as revealed in the gospel, and then that same gospel opens the way to touch every part of people's lives and the life of the city. Keep in mind that this is a church. The impact the church is having is far greater than what any individual could be doing. As a church, Redeemer's members are following Jesus and seeing that impact felt around the world. The impact that you will have through your own church may be different—but the gospel does change everything, starting with you, and it will make a difference in the world you touch.

Here is the first core value of Redeemer, which serves as a good way to conclude this lesson on gospel obedience:

> **The gospel changes everything.** The gospel is not the A-B-C's but the A–Z of Christianity. It is not just the minimum required doctrine for salvation, but it is the heart of and the point of all doctrine. The gospel is the hub in the "wheel" of truth. It is not just the entrance to the kingdom, but the way we make all progress (Gal. 3:1–3) and become renewed both individu-

3. The Web site of Redeemer Presbyterian Church can be found at http://www.redeemer.com.

ally (Col. 1:6), and socially (Gal. 2:14). The gospel renews us as we come to grips with our personal and corporate "idols." Idols are always alternative works-salvation ways of avoiding Christ's grace-salvation. Psychologically, all despair, guilt, fear, and anger come to the degree that something besides Jesus and his grace (career, family, moral performance, romance) is operating as our functional savior. Sociologically, all injustice, violence, strife, dependency, intolerance come to the degree that something besides Jesus and his grace (wealth, race/blood, the state, human reason) is operating as our functional savior.[4]

Summary of Chapter 11

Gospel obedience means that we join with Jesus on his mission. *We are missionaries!* This means that:

- We learn to view all of life as being under the lordship of Christ.
- We participate in Jesus' work to send the gospel to all nations.

We are called to the renewal of our minds. A Christian worldview should lead to a Christian lifestyle, affecting everything we do. Consider examples of Christian worldview and lifestyle:

- God's purpose for earthly government.
- Use of money and possessions.
- Vocation.
- Care for the weak.

4. Class notes, "Redeemer: A Gospel Driven Church Model."

The call to discipleship in our daily lives is the call to understand that *the gospel changes everything*.

Assignments

1. **Keep reading your Bible regularly.** Make sure that you have completed reading Romans and Acts. Prepare for the next lesson by reading Paul's letter to Titus.
2. **Think and write about your sense of vocation.** Review the three ideas of calling as it looks in your life. Specifically, what is your calling at this point to serve Christ in the world?
3. **Begin to think about ministry after this study.** In the next lesson we will talk about your participating in Jesus' great work of taking the gospel to all nations, including our own families and communities. You need to begin prayerfully thinking about specific steps you could begin to take. More about this next time.

PART THREE

FOLLOWING JESUS ON HIS MISSION

We cannot study discipleship or answering the call of Jesus to follow him without asking ourselves, "Where is this going?" To finish the study, we need a lesson on the purpose or mission of disciples of Jesus. Simply stated, *we are called to carry on the mission that Jesus began.*

CHAPTER 12

Disciples Making Disciples

WHATEVER HAPPENED TO TITUS?

We began our study of discipleship by looking at a young man in Rome named Titus. I chose that name deliberately because a man named Titus in the New Testament was one of Paul's companions in ministry. By the end of Paul's ministry he was one of his most trusted workers, and was even assigned the task of establishing the church on the island of Crete, as you read in Paul's letter to him (Titus 1:4–5). He was not the same person as our Titus, but he is a model of what I hope happened to our Titus, and more importantly what I pray happens to every disciple who has been doing this study. Take a few minutes and review where our lessons have taken us:

- Like Titus, we all begin as those who feel drawn to Jesus. I think it is only as we look back that we realize we were being *called* by Jesus. It was a call that came through the gospel to repent and believe in Jesus for salvation.

- The call to salvation is also a call to follow Jesus as his disciple. Don't forget the lesson that *disciple* is another way to describe a *believer* or a *Christian*. You saw this in your reading of Acts, where the common word for those who had come to believe in Jesus was *disciple*. And it was in one of the new churches, in the city of Antioch, that the disciples started to be called "Christians" (Acts 11:21, 26).

- Many extraordinary blessings belong to those who are following Jesus because of his call. We have looked at *justification*, *sanctification*, *adoption*, and *glorification*. Each of these is an unfolding of the "righteousness of God" revealed in the gospel (Rom. 1:17) and received by faith.

- Discipleship involves a total surrender to become "living sacrifices" (12:1). We are called to the "obedience that comes from faith" (1:5; 16:26), which can also be summarized as "faith expressing itself through love" (Gal. 5:6).

- Disciples of Jesus are missionaries. When Jesus called those first disciples, it was to follow him *on his mission*. One meaning of that mission, as we saw in the previous lesson, is to live out the Christian worldview in our daily lives in the world.

- Following Jesus on his mission also means that his disciples are now participating in the plan of God to bring all nations into the light of the gospel. Think of it this way: We who were called to follow Jesus as his disciples are ourselves now called to "make disciples" (Matt. 28:19). This is what I mean by "disciples making disciples."

MAKE DISCIPLES OF ALL NATIONS

When the writers of the four gospel accounts tell us the story of Jesus, they all emphasize the centrality of the cross and resurrection. The great plan of God to bring peace and salvation to the broken world could happen only because the Son of God went to the cross as "the Lamb of God, who takes away the sin of the world" (John 1:29). But once he had been raised from the dead, Jesus immediately focused on the mission that was now possible because of what he had done. His first words to the assembled disciples following his resurrection were these: "Just as the Father sent me, even so I am sending you" (John 20:21, a literal translation). In other words, Jesus was passing along to his disciples the mission that had been given to him by his Father.

On another occasion Jesus was with the disciples in Galilee, which was the home district of most of the first disciples. Some of them were still struggling to understand what was going on ("some doubted," Matt. 28:17), but Jesus spoke words that have become known as the *Great Commission*. It is very important to try to understand this passage.

Read Your Bible: Matthew 28:16–20

Did you notice that the Great Commission begins and ends with Jesus speaking of *his authority* (v. 18) and *his presence* (v. 20)? This means that there is no thought that we are on our own in the calling to "make disciples of all nations" (v. 19). One of the great prophecies of the work of Messiah is Isaiah 49:6, "I will also make you a light for the Gentiles [nations], that you may bring my salvation to the ends of the earth." That mission is being carried out right now—but it is being done by his disciples going in his power.[1]

Look carefully at the four key words of the Great Commission: *go*, *make disciples*, *baptizing*, *teaching*. The central command is to *make disciples*. The other three words explain *how* we are to make disciples.

By going. The idea is not necessarily that we must go away from home, but that we are dedicated to this mission. The word that some use for this idea is *intentional*. It is not only overseas missionaries or preachers who make disciples, but *all* disciples are to be involved in making more disciples. Look around to see how you can become involved in the lives of those near you at home and work.

By "baptizing them in the name of the Father and of the Son and of the Holy Spirit." The first phase of being a disciple, as we have studied, is coming to the place where we are ready to publicly confess Jesus before others. This is part of our *conversion*, and the work of leading people toward conversion is usually called *evangelism*. This understanding of evangelism is fine as long as it is not thought of as something different from making disciples. In practice the Great Commission is read, too often, as a command to go and make *converts*, which is not at all what Jesus commanded. Churches all over the world are full of people who confess to be Christians, who have perhaps prayed a prayer for salvation, but who seem to have no concept of being a disciple. If those in the church properly understood the Great Commission and preached a gospel that

1. Notice Acts 13:47, where Paul quotes the same text to support his calling to preach the gospel to the Gentiles.

called men and women to discipleship, we could begin to see that problem corrected.

By *"teaching them to obey everything I have commanded you."* Public confession of Jesus Christ as Lord and Savior and a life of obedience to his teaching are the two key elements of making disciples. This is *discipleship through the gospel*, both before and after coming to faith. The first steps of living in obedience to Jesus' teaching begin *before* we confess him, because in his call, Jesus commands us to repent, believe the gospel, and follow him. We continue and grow as disciples by staying focused on Jesus and learning what he is calling us to do. This is why the essential work of our churches is to be making disciples. It is not one "program" of the church, but the essence of its mission.

For Reflection

Stop and think about the disciples of Jesus who have been part of your discipleship. Who pointed you to Christ? Were there some who stayed involved in your life as you struggled to believe and follow Jesus? Who helped you grow as a disciple? Those people were "disciples making disciples." You may feel quite inadequate to be such a person yourself, but will you start by telling the Lord that with his strength, you are one of those willing to "go"? Talk about this with some others.

PARTNERSHIP IN THE GOSPEL

When we understand that making disciples is the mission of the whole church, then it means that we are not being asked to do everything. The idea of spiritual gifts we have studied applies to the Great Commission as well. A good example is the way in which the apostle Paul involved churches in his mission of going to Gentiles who had never heard of Jesus. He called this "partnership in the gospel" when he wrote to the church of Philippi (Phil. 1:5). Paul viewed their prayer and financial support as an investment in the work of the gospel, and any fruit he had was theirs as well. The church at home was just as important, in his view, as the work on the front line of gospel expansion (4:14–19).

The last reading we will do in Romans reveals more about Paul's plan to visit Rome. In chapter 1 he told them he was coming, but in chapter 15 he gives more detail. Paul was writing from Greece and was taking an offering from the churches of Macedonia and Achaia (two regions of Greece) to needy believers in Jerusalem. After that visit, he anticipated sailing west from Jerusalem to Rome and then on to his next mission—Spain. From your reading of Acts, you learned that God changed Paul's plan, but he did eventually get to Rome, even though he got there as a prisoner of the Roman government. Hints in the last books he wrote suggest that Paul did some other traveling (1 Tim. 1:3; Titus 1:3; 3:12), so that may very well have included his desired visit to Spain (Paul was a very determined man!).

Read Your Bible: Romans 15:23–33

Paul was the missionary going to make disciples in Spain, and he was expecting the church in Rome to join him in this ministry in at least three ways that we can still emulate today:

They would bless and refresh him (15:29, 32). It means a great deal when churches are enthusiastic in their support and encouragement of the frontline missionaries. When you take the time to hear about what missionaries are doing, and get to know them, perhaps even traveling to where they work, it is received by them as a great gift.

They would support him financially (15:24). Notice that assisting Paul on his journey to Spain was in the context of the offering that other believers had given to the poor of Jerusalem. Contributing money to support those in missions began with women and others who supported Jesus (Luke 8:1–3). It is a wonderful way to use the money God gives you to give away, and every church should be very much involved in contributing to the expansion of the gospel. Paul didn't mind asking the believers in Rome for that kind of practical help. Begin to contribute to your church's outreach ministries, but at some point you will also want to become personally involved in supporting the ministry of others.

They would pray for him (Rom. 15:30–32). Paul's struggle to get to Jerusalem and then to Rome would be helped by the prayers of the church. He told the Philippian church that their prayers for him joined with "the help given by the Spirit of Jesus Christ" would give him deliverance (Phil. 1:19). This is how much he valued the prayers of people in the churches. It points to the great mystery of prayer—that our feeble words actually contribute to the work of Jesus in the world. Begin to pray for the work of gospel advancement throughout the world. In time you will come to know people who visit or who go out from your church, and you can join their ministry through prayer in a much more personal way. This is part of praying "thy kingdom come; thy will be done on earth as it is in heaven."

Time Out

I still feel very inadequately equipped to "make disciples."

Can you make soup?

A church I formerly served as pastor hosted a wonderful ministry called *Christianity Explored* that introduces people to Jesus using the Gospel of Mark.[1] The ministry begins each evening with a dinner for people who are coming directly from work. There were those in the church who felt inadequate to talk or to host one of the tables, but they faithfully came each week and made soups and stews for the whole group. During the weeks of *CE*, several people would feel more and more drawn to Jesus. This led to conversions and public confessions of faith. Would you agree that those who helped by setting up tables or making soup were an important part of this example of making disciples? Of course they were. When our heart's desire is to see people transformed by the power of the gospel, then God will take that desire and find many ways to put us to work in his great plan of salvation.

It was also interesting to see that the helpers in the kitchen frequently entered into conversations with their dinner guests about Jesus. Although they didn't think they could "witness" in some formal sense, they were happy to talk about what Jesus was doing in their lives. In other words, they were "witnessing" just by being themselves.

1. Learn more about this ministry at www.christianityexplored.org.

BACK TO JERUSALEM

At the "beginning of the gospel" (Mark 1:1), there was only Jesus. Then Jesus called four others, then still others. By the time Jesus ascended to his Father in heaven, there were 120 believers who assembled to hear Peter (Acts 1:15). A few days later he poured out the Holy Spirit to baptize his church, and immediately three thousand were added to their number (2:41). Soon it was five thousand (4:4). Yet the total number of believers was even greater than that because many of the original believers had returned to their homes in other parts of the world, which may be how the church of Rome got started. As the disciples started to scatter, their number kept multiplying. I like to think of Jesus pouring out the Holy Spirit on his church by picturing him in heaven tipping over a massive vat of honey. It fell on the disciples in Jerusalem but then slowly spread in a larger and larger circle. It is a pool of gospel honey bringing sweetness to a sour world. And what happened in Jerusalem, on the seventh Sunday after the first Easter, called Pentecost, was the beginning of something that is still going on. The gospel is moving out farther and farther, as it will until the day promised in the Old Testament when the earth "will be full of the knowledge of the LORD as the waters cover the sea" (Isa. 11:9).

Read Your Bible: Acts 1:1–11

This is another example of Jesus' teaching about his mission after doing what only he could do (his "suffering," 1:3). Luke, the author of Acts, begins by saying that in his first book (the gospel according to Luke) he "wrote about all that Jesus *began* to do and to teach" (1:1). The little word *began* makes it clear that what Luke will write about in Acts is to be understood as what Jesus will *continue* "to do and to teach"—only now Jesus is doing this through his church, baptized with the Holy Spirit (1:4–8). Remember that Jesus did not begin his ministry until the Father had baptized him with the Holy Spirit (Mark 1:8–11), and now Jesus would do the same thing for his disciples. They were to wait for that baptism (which came just a few days later on the day of Pentecost, Acts 2), and then, starting in Jerusalem, they would go out to the surrounding communities in Judea and Samaria and then to the ends of the earth, to be his witnesses.

The story of the growth of Jesus' followers is one of the most remarkable that could be imagined. Two thousand years after Pentecost, 2.1 billion people call themselves Christians. That is about one-third of the population of the earth, and the church continues to expand rapidly. That is not to judge how many of the 2.1 billion have genuine faith, but it does demonstrate that Jesus' mission to take the gospel to all nations of the earth is being fulfilled. The number of human failures, feeble churches, and misdirected disciples seems to make it clear that this extraordinary growth is not the result of human planning and effort. God is fulfilling his eternal plan of salvation. The gospel is *still* the "power of God for the salvation of everyone who believes" (Rom. 1:16).

Perhaps the most amazing demonstration of the work of gospel expansion in the modern era has been the church of China. It was *after* missionaries were expelled by the Communists in 1949 and *after* efforts were made to eradicate all believers in the "cultural revolution" of the 1960s that the number of believers in China virtually exploded. Today a conservative estimate of the Christian believers in China is *54 million*. The church in China is still under persecution, and there are many problems and needs. Nevertheless, among Chinese believers there is a missionary movement called "Back to Jerusalem." That phrase comes from the observation that the gospel has seemed to move from Jerusalem to the West. It went from the Middle East to Africa and Europe, then to the Americas, and from America to the Far East, especially Korea and China. So the vision of the Chinese is that they be used of God to complete the movement of the gospel around the globe until it once again gets to Jerusalem. Just like my illustration of the pool of gospel honey, "Back to Jerusalem" doesn't tell the whole story, but it is a wonderful expression of the vision of Jesus' disciples to obey his Great Commission to *make disciples of all nations.*

Summary of Chapter 12

What happened to Titus? There is a Titus in the New Testament who became a believer and then grew as a disciple until he was one of Paul's trusted assistants. That is the picture of the kind of growth that I pray will be true for all doing this study.

The Great Commission given by Jesus after his resurrection has the key command to "make disciples of all nations." The other key words tell us how to make disciples:

- By going (we are intentional about making disciples).
- By baptizing (evangelism is the first stage of making disciples, not a separate activity).
- By teaching to obey all things Jesus has taught (making disciples includes both confessing Christ publicly and living a life of obedience).

Partnership in the gospel is illustrated by Paul's trip to Rome and then to Spain, providing a good example of how a church can be involved in the work of the missionary who is making disciples on the front line of gospel expansion:

- By blessing and refreshing them.
- By supporting them financially.
- By praying for them.

"Back to Jerusalem," the story of how the gospel went from Jerusalem out into the world is remarkable, and it is still going on. The gospel will spread out to the nations until the knowledge of the Lord covers the earth. Jesus' disciples have been imperfect, but the plan of God is being fulfilled.

A Final Word to New and Renewed Followers of Jesus: Now What?

WE HAVE COME to the end of our study of discipleship for new and renewed disciples. If you are still doing this study, I have to assume that you are not in the same place in your spiritual journey as you were when we began. I'm sure you appreciate the fact that the call to follow Jesus is something we will observe all our lives. It is not completed by reading this or any other book or course of study. This means that you will have taken a few more steps in your walk, but this is hardly the end. I pray that you will continue to grow in your knowledge and love of Jesus, in your understanding of the Bible, in your commitment to the body of Christ, and in your vocation to serve Christ in the particular job that he has given you to do in the world.

Look over Appendix A, "Further Reading," which follows, and begin a course of reading that will deepen your understanding of what we have studied. You also need to find time to work your way through the readings on the life of Christ in Appendix B. I also want to recommend a book of meditations

I wrote called *Forty Days on the Mountain*.[1] The meditations are based on my study of Moses meeting God on Mount Sinai. I encourage you to study this book because it will serve as a good introduction to reading the Old Testament, and it will deepen your relationship with God.

But my major aim as we conclude this study is to challenge you to consider how you can be personally involved as a disciple in making more disciples. I believe that if you ask God in prayer to use you in the lives of others, he will answer that prayer. And before you get great visions of faraway places, prayerfully consider the opportunities that are close by:

- Discipleship must begin at home. If you have children, your first mission is to point them to Jesus. Do you pray as a family? Do you pray with your spouse? Because you are with your family constantly, discipleship in the home will be "caught" more than "taught," but you need to understand that the "go" of the Great Commission isn't necessarily sending you far away.
- How are you loving fellow disciples in your church community? If you pray that you will find someone to encourage in your church, you will discover plenty of needy people around you every Sunday. Making disciples happens in a church as people take an interest in one another and sincerely want to be part of others' spiritual growth.
- Find a ministry through your church or in the community through which you can learn to serve others. What

1. Stephen Smallman, *Forty Days on the Mountain: Meditations on Knowing God* (Wheaton, IL: Crossway Books, 2007).

are your gifts, your strengths, your weaknesses? Pray for a place where you "fit," and follow Jesus in loving your neighbor.

- Don't become so church-oriented, however, that you neglect the opportunities to be Christ's disciple where you work or go to school. There are many troubling things in the world we live in, but no one knows how much worse they would be without the servants of Christ quietly serving and loving others. The world has changed because of the prayers and efforts of Christ's disciples. Pray that you will be one of those change-makers.

- And finally, why not pray that you can find someone or several others who will study this book with you? You may not think you are an "expert" yet, but if you have worked through *The Walk* with someone else leading you, why not try to do the same with others? Even if you have read the book by yourself, its lessons will mean more when talking and praying with others. You don't have to present yourself as the expert, but be honest and say that you need to relearn the same basic lessons yourself. Appendix C is a statement written to those who are involved in making disciples. You should find it helpful.

APPENDIX A

Further Reading and Resources

The Walk: Steps for New and Renewed Followers of Jesus was written as a guide to help you get started as a disciple of Jesus. You probably have many more questions than could be answered in the book, so here are several suggestions for reading material that can help you. Some of them have already been mentioned. I have arranged them in the order the topics were discussed in the book.

Questions You May Have before You Can Take the Call of Jesus Seriously

Timothy Keller, *The Reason for God: Belief in an Age of Skepticism* (New York: Dutton, 2008).
A book that asks and answers questions such as why people suffer, whether the Bible is reliable, and how the Bible and science can be compatible, and then also explains the reasons for faith.

C. S. Lewis, *Mere Christianity* (New York: Collier Books, 1960).
A classic explanation of the basic ideas of Christianity that first appeared in 1943 and has reappeared in many subsequent editions.

Lewis came to faith from a life of agnosticism, so he remembers his own struggles to believe.

Lee Strobel, *The Case for Christ* (Grand Rapids: Zondervan, 1998).
A journalist's description of his quest for truth about Jesus. In the course of his investigation, he interviews key scholars on the reliability of the New Testament accounts and the validity of teaching about Jesus. Strobel has written several other books that address basic questions.

PART ONE: THE BASICS

The Person of Jesus and the Gospel

Christianity Explored (www.christianityexplored.com).
A London-based ministry that is designed to guide churches in using the book of Mark to introduce people to Jesus. The ministry's Web site has many resources, including "Discipleship Explored."

Sinclair Ferguson, *Let's Study Mark* (Edinburgh: Banner of Truth Trust, 1999).
A very helpful study guide to take you through the gospel of Mark. Ferguson's writings are always biblically based and helpful.

Timothy Keller, *The Prodigal God* (New York: Dutton, 2008).
A book that starts with the parable of the prodigal son to explain the radical nature of the gospel message.

Paul Miller, *Love Walked among Us* (Colorado Springs: NavPress, 2001).
Stories from the Gospels about Jesus to introduce people to his life and ministry. The author, Paul Miller, is the son of Jack and

Rose Marie Miller. Learn more about Paul's ministry at his Web site: www.seeJesus.net.

The *Jesus* film (www.jesusfilm.org).
A widely distributed film that uses the gospel of Luke to convey the life and ministry of Jesus. Free copies are available through the Web site.

Scripture

Bibles and Bible translations (www.best-bible.org).
Reliable information about different Bible translations and study Bibles.

Bible study helps (www.crosswalk.com).
One of the most popular Web sites for help with research into Bible passages and background. Those who like to use the Web to do study will consult this resource often.

Tremper Longman III, *Reading the Bible with Heart and Mind* (Colorado Springs: NavPress, 1997).
A practical overview of the Bible and how to read and understand it.

Vaughan Roberts, *God's Big Picture: Tracing the Storyline of the Bible* (Nottingham, UK: IVP Books, 2002).
A helpful introduction to the kingdom theme of Scripture by selecting key passages for study and comment.

The ESV Study Bible (Wheaton, IL: Crossway Bibles, 2008).
The "Cadillac" of study Bibles, which uses the recent English Standard Version translation. It includes very helpful notes and maps, and excellent articles on Bible background, history, and biblical doctrines.

The NIV Study Bible (Grand Rapids: Zondervan, 1985).
A helpful study Bible for those who are reading the New International Version. This is the most popular study Bible of the most popular translation today.

The Church

Mark Dever, *The Deliberate Church: Building Your Ministry on the Gospel* (Wheaton, IL: Crossway Books, 2005).
A helpful introduction to the basics of being a church that stays focused on the essentials of a church's calling.

C. John Miller, *Outgrowing the Ingrown Church* (Grand Rapids: Zondervan, 1986).
Miller's story of his own transformation as a pastor, the beginnings of the New Life churches, and how that process applies to the life of any church.

PART TWO: DISCIPLESHIP THROUGH THE GOSPEL

Calling and Conversion

C. John Miller, *A Faith Worth Sharing* (Phillipsburg, NJ: P&R Publishing, 1999).
Miller's last book, completed by his wife, Rose Marie, in which he tells stories of his own conversion and his efforts to share his faith with others over the course of his life.

C. John Miller, *Repentance: A Daring Call to Real Surrender* (Fort Washington, PA: CLC Publications, 2009).

Miller's first book (first published as *Repentance and 20th Century Man*). It is an insightful and practical discussion of repentance both before and after conversion.

John Piper, *Finally Alive* (Ross-shire, Scotland: Christian Focus, 2009).
Very helpful and practical teaching on the meaning of the new birth. These lessons are very solidly based in study of Scripture as is all of the writing of John Piper. If you are not familiar with the ministry of John Piper and the helpful resources he makes available, check his website: www.desiringgod.org.

Redeemer Presbyterian Church, New York (www.redeemer.com/learn/resources).
Helpful resources on personal conversion and spiritual growth.

Stephen Smallman, *Spiritual Birthline: Understanding How We Experience the New Birth* (Wheaton, IL: Crossway Books, 2006); *What Is True Conversion?* (Phillipsburg, NJ: P&R Publishing, 2005).
My writing on conversion, emphasizing salvation as a process that is begun by the work of the Holy Spirit.

Gospel Doctrines

Jerry Bridges, *The Discipline of Grace* (Colorado Springs: NavPress, 1994).
A book that describes God's role and our role in the pursuit of holiness. Bridges is a godly and thoughtful author whose books are always practical and profitable.

Sinclair Ferguson, *The Christian Life: A Doctrinal Introduction* (Edinburgh: Banner of Truth Trust, 1981).
A wonderful study of the doctrines of salvation, including practical ways in which salvation by grace alone can be lived out.

C. J. Mahaney, *Living the Cross Centered Life* (Colorado Springs: Multnomah Books, 2006).
The leader of Sovereign Grace Ministries explains how to "keep the Gospel the main thing" in his own life and ministry.

R. C. Sproul, *Truths We Confess*, 3 vols. (Phillipsburg, NJ: P&R Publishing, 2006–07).
Sproul's "Laymen's Guide to the Westminster Confession of Faith." Sproul is a great Bible teacher and author whose writings are always meaty and trustworthy.

Milton Vincent, *A Gospel Primer for Christians* (Bemidji, MN: Focus Publishing, 2008).
A pastor's own story that explains how he preaches the gospel to himself every day.

World Harvest Mission (www.whm.org). Two programs for gospel renewal:
Gospel Transformation (36 weeks)
The Gospel-Centered Life (9 weeks)
The mission produces very helpful and practical materials that enable "an approach to discipling that centers on the transformation of Christians by believing the Good News." Designed to be helpful in small groups and church classes. Contact World Harvest directly.

Gospel Obedience/Worldview

Charles Colson, *The Faith: Given Once for All* (Grand Rapids: Zondervan, 2008).
An explanation of "What Christians Believe, Why They Believe It, and Why It Matters," using the outline of the Nicene Creed. This is the latest in a series of books that Colson has written to help Christians think "Christianly."

Charles H. Dunahoo, *Making Kingdom Disciples* (Phillipsburg, NJ: P&R Publishing, 2005).
A challenge to churches and their leaders to incorporate kingdom perspective into the discipleship and teaching ministries of the church.

Philip Graham Ryken, *What Is the Christian Worldview?* (Phillipsburg, NJ: P&R Publishing, 2006).
A very helpful booklet introducing the essentials of the Christian worldview.

PART THREE: FOLLOWING JESUS ON HIS MISSION

Disciples Making Disciples

Patrick Johnstone, *Operation World, 21st Century Edition* (Pasadena, CA: William Carey Library and Publishers, 2001).
An invaluable resource for learning about the spread of the gospel throughout the world. Information is provided country by country as an aid to systematic prayer for the advancement of the kingdom of Jesus Christ.

C. John Miller, *Powerful Evangelism for the Powerless* (Phillipsburg, NJ: P&R Publishing, 1997).
A revision of a book originally published as *Evangelism and Your Church* in 1980. Miller believed that true evangelism can take place only in the context of a vital congregation, and practiced this belief.

Jim Petersen, *Lifestyle Discipleship* (Colorado Springs: NavPress, 1993).
A book written by a vice president of the Navigators, a ministry devoted to discipleship. Petersen calls for a fresh look at discipleship and describes what it should look like. He stresses the importance of community, but does not focus on the local church as community.

APPENDIX B

"Sirs, We Would See Jesus"

A Fifteen-Week Reading Plan to Introduce the Life and Teachings of Jesus Christ

THE CONCEPT

The starting place of discipleship is to believe in Jesus. But we can believe in him without knowing much about him. So the Lord anointed four authors to each write a *gospel*—an account of Jesus' life and teachings to explain who he was and what it meant to follow him. The seventy-five readings that follow have been selected from the four gospels according to a generally agreed-upon outline that divides the adult life of Jesus into three years of ministry. This period began with events in the life of John the Baptist (his preaching, imprisonment, and death), but information was arranged differently by the authors, and the precise sequence of events is difficult to determine. A longer portion has been selected for personal reading, but we often suggest a briefer reading (in parentheses) for those who would like to use this resource for family worship and teaching that includes younger children. Regularly consulting a map of Palestine in the time of Jesus will make the readings much more meaningful.

I. The Year of Inauguration

WEEK 1

1. The ministry of John the Baptist—Luke 3:1–18 (Mark 1:1–8)
2. The baptism of Jesus—Matthew 3:13–17
3. The temptation of Jesus—Matthew 4:1–11
4. John's disciples as followers of Jesus—John 1:29–51 (1:35–42)
5. The first miracle—John 2:1–11

WEEK 2

1. Jesus' first ministry in Jerusalem—John 2:12–25
2. Teaching about the new birth—John 3:1–21 (3:1–8)
3. Witness to the Samaritan woman—John 4:1–42 (4:1–14)
4. Hometown rejection—Luke 4:14–30
5. Jesus' move to Capernaum—Luke 4:31–44

II. The Year of Popularity

WEEK 3

1. Sermon on the Mount: Calling of the first disciples—Matthew 4:12–25
2. Sermon on the Mount: Power to heal and forgive—Luke 5:12–26
3. Sermon on the Mount: The call of Levi (Matthew)—Luke 5:27–39 (5:27–32)
4. Sermon on the Mount: First conflict about the Sabbath—Luke 6:1–11

5. Sermon on the Mount: The twelve apostles named—Luke 6:12–16

WEEK 4

1. Sermon on the Mount: The Beatitudes—Matthew 5:1–16
2. Sermon on the Mount: Jesus and the Law—Matthew 5:17–30 (5:17–20)
3. Sermon on the Mount: Jesus and the Law (continued)—Matthew 5:31–48 (5:43–48)
4. Giving and prayer—Matthew 6:1–15
5. Fasting; treasure in heaven—Matthew 6:16–24

WEEK 5

1. Exhortation not to worry—Matthew 6:25–34
2. True judgment—Matthew 7:1–12
3. Entering at the narrow gate—Matthew 7:13–29
4. Second ministry in Jerusalem—John 5:1–15
5. Jesus' discourse on his divinity—John 5:16–47 (5:19–27)

WEEK 6

1. The faith of the centurion and widow—Luke 7:1–17
2. Questions from John the Baptist—Luke 7:18–35 (7:18–23)
3. Jesus and a sinful woman—Luke 7:36–50 (7:36–43)
4. The parable of the sower—Luke 8:1–15
5. Other parables of the kingdom—Matthew 13:24–43 (13:31–35)

WEEK 7

1. Jesus' calming of the storm—Mark 4:35–41
2. Healing of the Gadarene demoniac—Mark 5:1–20
3. A dead girl and a sick woman—Mark 5:21–43 (5:24–34)
4. Jesus rejected again—Matthew 13:47–58 (13:53–58)
5. Sending out of the disciples; death of John—Luke 9:1–9

III. The Year of Opposition

Week 8

1. Feeding the five thousand—Luke 9:10–17
2. Jesus' walk on water—Matthew 14:22–36
3. Jesus the Bread of Life—John 6:25–71 (6:35–40)
4. Clean and unclean—Matthew 15:1–28 (15:21–28)
5. Peter's confession—Matthew 16:13–28 (16:13–20)

Week 9

1. The Mount of Transfiguration—Matthew 17:1–23 (17:1–9)
2. The character of the kingdom—Matthew 18:1–20 (18:15–20)
3. The parable of the Good Samaritan—Luke 10:25–37
4. Teaching about prayer—Luke 10:38–11:13 (11:9–13)
5. Jesus and Beelzebub—Luke 11:14–28 (11:14–20)

Week 10

1. Jesus the Good Shepherd—John 10:1–42 (10:7–16)
2. Counting the cost—Luke 14:25–35
3. Parables of finding the lost—Luke 15:1–32 (15:3–10)
4. Entering the kingdom—Luke 18:9–30 (18:9–17)
5. The raising of Lazarus—John 11:1–44 (11:32–44)

IV. The Final Week and Resurrection Life

Week 11

1. Plots against Jesus—John 11:45–12:10 (12:1–10)
2. The triumphal entry—Matthew 21:1–17
3. Debates about authority—Matthew 21:23–46 (21:28–32)
4. Debates about priorities—Matthew 22:1–46 (22:34–40)
5. The Olivet Discourse—Luke 21:1–38 (21:1–4)

Week 12

1. The Last Supper—Matthew 26:14–35
2. Jesus' washing of the disciples' feet—John 13:1–30 (13:2–11)
3. Jesus' comforting of the disciples—John 13:31–14:14 (14:1–7)
4. Jesus' promise of the Holy Spirit—John 14:15–31 (14:15–21)
5. The Vine and the branches—John 15:1–27 (15:1–8)

Week 13

1. Jesus' High Priestly Prayer—John 17:1–26 (17:20–26)
2. Jesus in Gethsemane—Matthew 26:36–56 (26:36–46)
3. Jesus at the house of Caiaphas—Matthew 26:57–75 (26:69–75)
4. Jesus before Pilate—Matthew 27:1–26 (27:1–2, 19–26)
5. Jesus beaten and crucified—Matthew 27:27–53 (27:32–44)

Week 14

1. Jesus on the cross—Luke 23:26–43
2. Jesus' death and burial—John 19:28–42
3. Resurrection morning—Matthew 28:1–20 (28:1–10)
4. Mary's meeting with Jesus—John 20:1–18
5. Two on the road to Emmaus—Luke 24:13–35

Week 15

1. Jesus' first meeting with the disciples—John 20:19–31
2. Jesus on the shore of Galilee—John 21:1–25 (21:15–19)
3. Final days with Jesus—Acts 1:1–11
4. Jesus' promise kept—Acts 2:1–21 (2:1–13)
5. Jesus' living in his church—Acts 2:22–47 (2:42–47)

APPENDIX C

A Word to Disciples Who Are Involved in Making Disciples

As I noted in the preface, *The Walk: Steps for New and Renewed Followers of Jesus* started as a plan to write a book for individuals who might need helpful information for getting started on their Christian walk. The more I worked on it, however, the more I became convinced that the greater usefulness of this book could be as a resource to help disciples make other disciples. I have tried to write a guidebook, not a "fact" book. Discipleship is something that must be *lived*, not just studied. As Ron (who helped me to "field-test" this book) said to our little group, "Discipleship is primarily a lab course with a few lectures now and then." Well said! Many of us have tended to make it primarily lectures (or sermons), with very little help on the practice side. Furthermore, we must avoid the temptation to define discipleship as merely reading a book or completing a program.

It is my hope and prayer that *The Walk* will provide a useful tool to those of you who want to guide and encourage others who are hearing the call of Jesus to follow him. I'm thinking particularly of those of you who would never consider yourselves "disciple makers." Perhaps a step-by-step resource like this will encourage you to ask someone to do a study with you. And keep in mind that our involvement in making disciples will be one of the most significant things we can do for our own growth as disciples. This will be a challenging and exciting enterprise. To help you in this great mission, I'm adding this appendix with thoughts on two topics:

- Some of this book's distinctive emphases. My approach to discipleship has some fundamental issues that you need to appreciate as you use this book in your own discipleship ministry. I will also try to suggest several other resources that could help you grow in your understanding.
- Practical suggestions about how you might make use of this book.

UNDERLYING PRINCIPLES

The Great Commission does not make our modern distinction between evangelism and discipleship.

The fundamental premise of *The Walk* is a proper understanding of the Great Commission (Matt. 28:18–20). Any number of writers and teachers have demonstrated that the main command in the Great Commission is to *make disciples* (from the Greek verb *mathateuo*, which has the same root as *mathatas*, the word for *disciple*). As I explain in chapter 12, the other key words of the Great Commission (*go*, *baptizing*, and *teaching*) flesh out what is involved in making disciples. This means that your mandate is only beginning to unfold when you see people make a profession of faith. Furthermore, we must have this expectation of discipleship in view at the beginning of our work with people. Take time to review the scheme of evangelism that you or your church is involved in and ask whether it presents the gospel in a way that anticipates a life of following Jesus. If "going to heaven" is the key objective of evangelism, perhaps that begins to tell us why discipleship is viewed as optional by so many "converts."

I have appreciated the writing of the late Dr. Robert Webber in his *Ancient-Future* series of books. *Ancient-Future Evangelism: Making Your Church a Faith-Forming Community*[1] is particularly helpful. The author tries to use the experience of the early church and how it approached evangelism to teach us a more biblical understanding of evangelism and discipleship in the local church.

Discipleship is not a distinct category of Christian living, nor is it something in addition to believing.

This point grows naturally from a biblical understanding of the Great Commission, but it needs to be emphasized. I have tried to write in a way that assumes that believers are disciples. In my experience, those I classify as *new disciples* will accept this idea readily. It will be the established Christians, including pastors and other church leaders, who will find this a new thought. You need to think about this, and ask whether your understanding of the gospel includes discipleship, or whether you are one who views discipleship as a later stage of Christian living.

You may have noticed that I didn't begin my study with a discussion of salvation, but with discipleship. I did so because this is how Mark presents the gospel. Apparently those first disciples began their life of following Jesus by learning who he was and why he came. Were they "saved" when they began as disciples? Who can say? But clearly, as those who identified themselves as disciples of Jesus, they were involved in a process of discovery of what it meant to be saved by Jesus. I have assumed that the disciples of the church in Rome would also have experienced this process. The unpacking of the gospel that Paul

1. Grand Rapids: Baker Books, 2003.

does in Romans may have solidified the faith of believers, or it may have helped "seekers" understand what it meant to believe in Christ for salvation. But in either case, discipleship as the normal response of faith would have been assumed.

As you begin a study of *The Walk*, don't focus on whether or not the people you are studying with are believers in Jesus. That will become evident as you have discussions, and there will be also ample opportunity to pursue this matter once you get to chapters 5 and 6.[2]

Discipleship begins with the call of Jesus, not a person's decision.

I am convinced that one major reason that some teachers and leaders in the church have difficulty stressing discipleship, even in their presentation of the gospel, is the assumption that discipleship begins with our choice to follow. There is such a passion to avoid even the suggestion that salvation is a result of our works, or effort to earn God's favor, that evangelists place a heavy and constant emphasis on the fact that we can't earn and don't deserve salvation. I have even heard many well-meaning evangelists speak of how *easy* it is to become a Christian. They so studiously avoid anything that suggests effort, other than a faith commitment or "decision for Jesus," that any thought of "take up [your] cross and follow me" (Mark 8:34) is a matter to be considered *after* responding to the gospel.

But if we have a different starting point, then we can expect a very different set of responses and outcomes. The call to discipleship begins with just that—the call. When Jesus called those first disciples, they followed, because they were encountering Jesus, the Son of God, whose call included the power to respond. This fact came home to me with new force in rereading the early chapters of Dietrich

2. How to work with others is Part II of my book *Spiritual Birthline*, called "The Work of a Spiritual Midwife" (Wheaton, IL: Crossway Books, 2006).

Bonhoeffer's classic work, *The Cost of Discipleship*.[3] It coincided with my own studies and writing on the effectual call of the Holy Spirit, and I realized that Jesus' call to discipleship is essentially the same as the call to salvation that Paul and Peter mention over and over. That idea became the title of chapter 5 in this book. In other words, when we understand that people come to Christ because of the call (1 Cor. 1:18–31), then we will also understand that what is drawing them is Jesus himself, at whatever the cost, not the person's own expectation of a better life or a free gift.

In my reading of books and other studies of discipleship, I find that this emphasis on the supernatural call of God is usually only briefly mentioned, if at all. That makes discipleship (as well as evangelism) a largely human effort. I believe that what I have explained in terms of emphasizing the call of God as fundamental to the whole matter of discipleship is a needed emphasis, and I hope you find it helpful and encouraging—this is God's work we are involved in. You may want to give particular attention to the material in chapters 5 and 6. If you are acquainted with the theology of my tradition (Reformed and Presbyterian), you have probably heard the simple phrase "regeneration precedes faith" (that is, the work of God makes possible our response). In *The Walk* I have tried to make a practical application of this truth in the way a person carries out ministry.

Don't assume that people understand the gospel, in terms of either experience or theology.

When I tell people that I am trying to write about "discipleship for dummies," I frequently get smiles in return and then an immediate word of encouragement for this endeavor. There seems to be a widespread recognition that even in our established church, a great many believers are uncertain about the basics. So in whatever setting

3. Dietrich Bonhoeffer, "Costly Grace," "The Call to Discipleship," chaps. 1, 2 in *The Cost of Discipleship* (1937; repr. New York: Touchstone, 1995).

you use this book, don't assume that those in your group understand even the gospel, which supposedly "everybody" knows. No, they don't! This is particularly true when discipleship is assumed as part of the gospel itself, not something for later. Pray for sensitivity, whether you are working with those who are very new or those who have been around for a while.

Keep in mind also that people can sincerely believe the gospel, as they understand it (what is often labeled "saving faith"), but that such an understanding can be very superficial. God alone knows whether such people are "saved," but the task of discipleship is just beginning. Take all the time you need to let the gospel sink in. One friend described the slow process of the gospel's penetrating our souls as being "pickled in the gospel."

The gospel is far more than a message for unbelievers.

If you have read this book, you know that I repeat this message over and over. My prayer is that for those who are new to the gospel, this idea will become second nature. But for those who are the "mature" or seasoned Christians in your midst, this may not come so easily. Church people will usually nod in agreement that they need the gospel, but in action and conversation it is clear that they follow the typical "saved by grace, grow by works" approach. Ironically, the reason they may be part of your group doing this study is that their approach to the Christian life just hasn't "worked." What doesn't work is trying to follow Jesus without Jesus' being at the core of their being.

I challenge those of you seeking to disciple others to ask yourselves whether this is true for you. The renewal ministry that was launched under Jack Miller's leadership had its greatest impact on pastors and missionaries (and their wives) who were carrying out "gospel ministry" but who didn't know how to live out the gospel themselves. Milton Vincent, a pastor in California, recently wrote a little book called *A Gospel Primer for Christians*, which includes his personal story of frustration and despair, even after years of "successful" ministry, until he came to a new appreciation of the gospel for his daily life.[4] Pastor Vincent specifically mentions the impact of reading *The Discipline of Grace* by Jerry Bridges,[5] in which he was introduced to the statement: "Preach the gospel to yourself every day."[6] The classic "textbook" for this gospel orientation is *Dynamics of Spiritual Life*.[7]

The teaching of gospel doctrine was fundamental to Paul's discipleship of new believers.

I wondered, as you might, whether diving into the "heavy" theology of Romans was the right direction for the new disciples for whom I am writing. But Paul didn't hesitate to do it, and neither should we. The response from those who have "tested" the book has been encouraging as well. I sensed that they recognized that they were just beginning to comprehend concepts such as justification, but at the same time they were able to follow the thinking of Paul, at least in its basic outline, on these important matters. I think you will also discover that by the time you get to those chapters in the book (particularly 7–9), your group members will be demonstrating real growth in their ability to work with Scripture texts. I have deliberately set up the lessons to focus on a few select passages rather than numerous proof-texts. Take time to work through the passages, and let the Bible speak, but don't expect total comprehension. Those same lessons, reviewed later after more experience as a disciple of Jesus, will become much more meaningful.

4. Milton Vincent, *A Gospel Primer for Christians* (Bemidji, MN: Focus Publishing, 2008).

5. Jerry Bridges, *The Discipline of Grace* (Colorado Springs: NavPress, 1994). Jerry provides a particularly helpful explanation of this problem on pages 19–27.

6. This statement probably originated with Martin Luther, but Jack Miller used it constantly, and Jerry Bridges acknowledges that he first heard it from Jack and adopted it to give focus to a practice that he had been observing for some time (ibid., 8, 25).

7. Richard F. Lovelace, *Dynamics of Spiritual Life: An Evangelical Theology of Renewal* (Downers Grove, IL: InterVarsity Press, 1979).

That is why we must return to the gospel constantly—there are greater and greater depths to be discovered.

I teach justification and sanctification as linked to the cross and resurrection of Jesus. To me, that is taking the story of the gospel—Christ's death and resurrection—and internalizing it by faith. This is the gospel *in us*: we are united with Christ in his death and united with him in his resurrection. This means that the meaning of the gospel doesn't stop with justification, which seems to be the case in many definitions of the gospel. The gospel story includes, of course, the resurrection of Jesus, and our appreciation of the meaning of the gospel in our lives must include sanctification as well as adoption and glorification.

A valuable study for you as a leader is to note the times Paul prays that the new believers would *know*. This includes not only knowing Christ in the relational sense, but also understanding who they are in Christ and all the benefits that belong to them because of God's love and grace. You can see this particularly in Ephesians (1:15–19; 3:14–19) and Colossians (1:9–13; 2:1–5). In fact, the very ordering of the chapters in those books makes it clear that the insight about who Christ is and the fullness that believers have in Christ, explained in the first chapters, is the foundation for the day-to-day living out of the new life in Christ outlined in the later chapters. Paul prays for the *knowing* that will lead to the *doing* (Colossians 1:9–10 is particularly clear on this order). We need to follow that same pattern in our discipleship of others.

Use the historic tools of discipleship.

I have deliberately incorporated into *The Walk* the three core teachings that have been used throughout most of the history of the Church: the Apostles' Creed (ch. 2), the Lord's Prayer (ch. 3), and the Ten Commandments (ch. 10). A wonderful example of how these three are woven into a systematic teaching of the faith is an early catechism of the Reformation, the Heidelberg Catechism (1563). It is very unfortunate that these seem to have been bypassed in contemporary discipleship training. I encourage you to take some extra time to actually memorize these three foundational teachings. Not only is it profitable in itself, but it also connects those you disciple to the larger Christian community.

There is no discipleship without community.

Keep in mind that this principle pertains to the initial phase of making disciples (evangelism) as well as the nurture of the believer. In seminars or classes I frequently ask people about their own experience. I ask how many of them came to faith pretty much on their own, versus how many came through first becoming involved to some degree with a Christian community (family, church, or small group). The vast majority identify the latter path. People typically need to see the gospel while they are hearing the gospel (or *in order to* hear the gospel).

Following Jesus must include following Jesus in his mission.

This important truth struck me with particular force as I reflected on Mark. From the very first words of his call to follow, Jesus made it clear that being his disciple had a purpose—a mission. Not only was Jesus proclaiming and demonstrating the presence of the kingdom, but he specifically told those he was calling that he would make them "fishers of men" (Mark 1:17). I introduced this theme in chapter 1 and then returned to it in the last two chapters. While the call to follow Jesus in his mission is segmented in the book, I hope you will find ways to build it into the entire course of your teaching of *The Walk*. This is likely to come up in discussions of the activities that group members are involved in. Use those times to keep the focus on ministry and reaching out. This shouldn't happen after the study is complete, but as part of the basics of discipleship.

Some thoughtful work is being done in tying together the church as community, and a rediscovery of the centrality of the kingdom as the work that this community is to be doing. Jack Miller's *Outgrowing the Ingrown Church*[8] is a practical starting point. I again commend Robert Webber's *Ancient-Future* series. The subtitle of his *Ancient-Future Evangelism* is *Making Your Church a Faith-Forming Community*, which is what we want to be doing. Webber offers a helpful insight that the three aspects of discipleship that stand out in the New Testament are *believing*, *belonging*, and *behaving*.[9] The term that brings together the threads of community, discipleship, and kingdom is *missional*.[10] We are called together to be the people of God following Jesus. That sense of our mission is to pervade everything we do as a church.

HOW TO USE THIS BOOK IN MAKING DISCIPLES

Be flexible; be creative.

This is the first and most important "rule." I'm well aware that many people are much more comfortable with an "out-of-the-box" program for discipleship. Those can be helpful, but that approach does not reflect life, and it is not discipleship. How you actually use this book will depend on you as a leader and, most importantly, knowing those you are seeking to guide into a life of discipleship. For example, I'm aware of friends who invited some young adults to read through a manuscript of this book with them. They were so new to serious

8. C. John Miller, *Outgrowing the Ingrown Church* (Grand Rapids: Zondervan, 1986).

9. Robert E. Webber, *Ancient-Future Evangelism* (Grand Rapids: Baker Books, 2003), 72.

10. Three more academic works on the nature of the church and its mission that I have found helpful are these: Tod E. Bolsinger, *It Takes a Church to Raise a Christian* (Grand Rapids: Brazos Press, 2004); Darrell L. Guder, *The Continuing Conversion of the Church* (Grand Rapids: Eerdmans, 2000); Craig Van Gelder, *The Essence of the Church* (Grand Rapids: Baker Books, 2000).

consideration of Jesus that all agreed that they needed to take more time studying Mark together. I hope they are able to move on, and I'm offering a path to follow, but it is far more important that these young adults meet Jesus, however long it takes.

The relational element will be just as important as, if not more important than, the content of this book.

When I have asked Christian leaders about their own "discipleship" experiences, most of them recall not the content of what was studied, but the fact that people took time to love them and point them to Jesus. This is not to diminish the content of this book, but if you are ready to make a significant commitment of your time and energy to making disciples, those you disciple will never forget that. The time you use in your group meetings to get to know the members and develop the relationship must be considered as fundamental to your gatherings, not mere preliminaries.

The Walk *could be used as a Sunday school class, but . . .*

One of the reasons the book has twelve chapters is that it fits into a typical adult Sunday school unit of study. I wrote with that in mind, but after writing and then testing it on a Sunday school group, I'm not convinced that this is the best way to use it. The group I have been working with has been very diligent in doing their assignments, but that zeal is not typical of Sunday-morning classes. Our time together is definitely too short, and continuity has been difficult because of members' vacations and other reasons for missing class. Nevertheless, our group has been enthusiastic, and I believe there has been real spiritual growth. But the potential for using this book as a resource for discipleship has been only partially realized, in my view.

The ideal use of *The Walk* would probably be in a group of two or three or four who would commit to meeting regularly for up to a year. The meetings should be set for every third or fourth week so that ample time could be devoted to completing the assignments. An evening (or other mutually agreeable block of time) would be set aside to begin with review of the assignments, including notes in the group members' journals about Bible reading, personal reflections, and some assigned tasks. Then time would be given to a study and discussion of the chapter to be read for the week. I have tried to build a pattern of review into most chapters, but you may need more time for that. As people became more comfortable with the idea of prayer, the meeting should conclude with a time of intercession for one another.

While I was pastor of McLean Presbyterian Church (in the Washington, D.C. area), we developed a ministry called *Living for the King* (LFK) that involved the kind of evening I just described. People committed one night a week from September through May. That commitment included a readiness to read assigned books and other materials and to follow through with specified tasks. Much of the material in this book was developed while I led LFK. Over the years of LFK the numbers steadily grew, and we subdivided into small groups for the accountability portion of the evening. I have been away from McLean for several years, and I still regularly encounter people who tell me that LFK was a major turning point in their spiritual journeys. Ed Satterfield, who served as our associate pastor at the time, agrees with me that of all our church responsibilities, LFK was the most fulfilling.

I mention my experience with LFK because it is possible, even in our busy world, to find people ready to devote serious time to learn what it means to follow Jesus. Whatever framework you follow, pray for God to bring across your path those he is calling.

Never forget that you are part of God's accomplishing his purposes.

We are part of something far bigger than ourselves and far greater than anything we alone can accomplish. God's kingdom has come in the person of the King, Jesus. God's kingdom is coming as the Holy Spirit brings people into the kingdom by his regenerating power. This is happening all over the world as Jesus does exactly what he said he would do: "I will build my church" (Matt. 16:18). This is God himself at work, but amazingly, we have the extraordinary privilege of being part of what God is doing.

Because God is the one who makes the real changes, we must also be realistic about what we can do. We are to be available and committed, but we must guard against trying to do the work that only the Spirit can do. We don't want people to follow us. We want them to be disciples of Jesus.